Decentralized Business

A Guide to Transforming Business Strategies with Distributed Ledger Technologies

Gaurav Deshmukh
Syed Mohamed Thameem Nizamudeen

Apress®

Decentralized Business: A Guide to Transforming Business Strategies with Distributed Ledger Technologies

Gaurav Deshmukh
Tarzana, CA, USA

Syed Mohamed Thameem Nizamudeen
Austin, TX, USA

ISBN-13 (pbk): 979-8-8688-0952-1
ISBN-13 (electronic): 979-8-8688-0953-8
https://doi.org/10.1007/979-8-8688-0953-8

Managing Director, Apress Media LLC: Welmoed Spahr
Acquisitions Editor: Shivangi Ramachandran
Development Editor: James Markham
Editorial Assistant: Jessica Vakili

Cover designed by eStudioCalamar

Cover image designed by Isaac

Distributed to the book trade worldwide by Springer Science+Business Media New York, 1 New York Plaza, Suite 4600, New York, NY 10004-1562, USA. Phone 1-800-SPRINGER, fax (201) 348-4505, e-mail orders-ny@springer-sbm.com, or visit www.springeronline.com. Apress Media, LLC is a California LLC and the sole member (owner) is Springer Science + Business Media Finance Inc (SSBM Finance Inc). SSBM Finance Inc is a **Delaware** corporation.

For information on translations, please e-mail booktranslations@springernature.com; for reprint, paperback, or audio rights, please e-mail bookpermissions@springernature.com.

Apress titles may be purchased in bulk for academic, corporate, or promotional use. eBook versions and licenses are also available for most titles. For more information, reference our Print and eBook Bulk Sales web page at http://www.apress.com/bulk-sales.

Any source code or other supplementary material referenced by the author in this book is available to readers on GitHub. For more detailed information, please visit https://www.apress.com/gp/services/source-code.

If disposing of this product, please recycle the paper

Identity Verification....45
Decentralized Applications (dApps)....45
Tokenization....46
Voting Systems....47
Healthcare....47
Financial Services....47
Internet of Things (IoT)....48
Real-World Implementations....48
Chapter 5: Integrating DLTs in Cloud-Based Infrastructures....53
Identifying the Use Case....54
Choosing the Right DLT Platform....54
Ethereum (ETH)....55
Hyperledger Fabric....57
Corda....58
Quorum....59
Designing the DLT Network....59
Develop Smart Contracts....60
Testing and Validating....61
Deploy and Monitor....62
Architecture Considerations and Best Practices....64
Chapter 6: Challenges and Security....67
Technical Challenges of Decentralized Systems....68
Scalability....68
Interoperability....70
Consensus Mechanism....72
Privacy and Confidentiality....74

Security Risks and Mitigation Strategies....76
51% Attacks....76
Smart Contract Vulnerabilities....78
Sybil Attacks....80
Data Tampering....82
Chapter 7: Web3 Strategies for Cloud Professionals....85
Strategic Opportunities for Cloud Professionals....86
Creation of dApps....86
Smart Contracts....88
Development of Digital Assets....90
New Ownership and Transactional Models....90
Decentralized Storage....90
Decentralized Identity Management....93
Decentralized Computing....93
Decentralized Finance....93
Decentralized Governance....93
How to Excel in Decentralized Systems....94
Career Prospects in Web3 (for Cloud Professionals)....96
DLT Cloud Engineer....96
Smart Contract Developer....96
DLT Cloud Architect....96
DLT Security Specialist....97
DLT Consultant....97
Chapter 8: Case Studies....99
Estonia's eID System....101
Honduras' Public Land Record System....102

Supply Chain Management 104
Walmart's Food Tracking System 104
Financial Services 105
Ornua: Substituting LCs 105
Election Voting Systems 107
Utah County's Blockchain-Based Voting System 107
Healthcare 109
Medchain 109
Smart Contracts 110
Smart Contracts in Freight Invoice Management 110
Tokenization 111
Tokenization in Asset Ownership 111
dApps 112
Cloud Providers Integrating DLTs 113
Success Factors and Lessons Learned from Decentralization and Integrating DLTs into Business Operations 115
Success Factors 115
Lessons Learned 116

Chapter 9: Regulatory Considerations in Decentralized Cloud Solutions 119

User-Controlled Data Sharing 119
Consent Management 121
Transparency and Auditing 122
Data Privacy 123
Jurisdictional Issues 125
Decentralized Identity Management 127
Smart Contract Regulations 128

Chapter 10: Future Trends 131

Edge Computing 132

Decentralized Data Network 133

Serverless Computing 135

Cloud-Native Applications 137

Hybrid Cloud Strategies 138

The Future 140

Chapter 11: Conclusion..143

The Dawn of a Decentralized Future 143

Charting a Course Through Decentralized Cloud Solutions 144

Embracing the Future: Trends Shaping Web3 and Cloud 145

Sailing Through the Web3 Frontier 146

Index 147

About the Authors

Gaurav Deshmukh is a highly skilled technology leader with over a decade of experience driving transformative software engineering initiatives. Throughout his career, he has held pivotal technical roles at prominent companies such as Guidewire, Cigna, Home Depot, American Agricultural Laboratory (AmAgLab), Tata Elxsi, and Amdocs. Gaurav's expertise encompasses a range of cutting-edge technologies, including cloud computing, cybersecurity, software automation, data engineering, and full-stack development with various programming languages and web technology frameworks. He employs his vast knowledge to create innovative solutions that optimize workflows and drive business growth.

Gaurav holds both an MBA and a master's degree in Computer Science, with a focus on data warehousing and computer vision. He is dedicated to elevating the strategic role of software engineering in delivering business value. As a distinguished leader, Gaurav can be reached at gauravkdeshmukh89@gmail.com to explore transformative technical initiatives.

Syed Mohamed Thameem Nizamudeen is a distinguished information technology leader with a rich history of leadership roles at Oracle, Ernst & Young (EY), and PricewaterhouseCoopers (PWC). His expertise lies in cloud computing, cloud security, big data, machine learning, AI, and application modernization, where he applies his vast knowledge to pioneer innovative solutions.

Syed has worked with C-Suite executives of Fortune 100 firms in the past advising them on their application modernization efforts in aspects of IaaS, PaaS, SaaS, cloud security, multi-cloud, and Internet of Things during his tenure with reputed technology advisory firms—PricewaterhouseCoopers and Ernst & Young. Syed is committed to advancing technology's role in shaping the business landscape. Syed can be reached at smthameem@gmail.com.

CHAPTER 1

Introduction

Decentralized Business in the Web3 Era

Web 3.0 marks a transformative period in the world of technology. With Web3 already being a revolutionary aspect of the Internet, it focuses on empowering the user with enhanced liberty, decentralization, and security. As the years pass, it is changing the way users interact with the digital world and conduct business.

For some people, Web 3.0 might be an unfamiliar concept, even if they have interacted with it. The term was first introduced by the founder of HTTP, Tim Berners-Lee. He described "Web 3.0" as an integrated communication framework in which Internet data is machine-readable across different applications and systems. Meanwhile, the earliest version of the Internet, "Web 1.0," largely consisted of content consumers and web developers that dealt primarily with text or graphical content. It wasn't linked to any database but a static file system, which explained why there was little interaction on web pages. However, with the advent of "Web 2.0," the use of developers changed. It allowed users to participate in the creation process, limiting the need for developers. Web 2.0 enabled users to create and share massive categories of content worldwide.

G. Deshmukh and S. M. Thameem Nizamudeen, *Decentralized Business*,
https://doi.org/10.1007/979-8-8688-0953-8_1

Figure 1-1. *Tim Berners-Lee*

Tim Berners-Lee[1] imagined that when Web 3.0 is introduced, it will mark the integration of artificial intelligence (AI) and machine learning (ML). This will signify a mechanism where computers will be able to analyze and process data in the same manner as humans. This, in fact, allowed the arrival of an intelligent generation. It also facilitates the distribution of valuable content specifically catered to the user's needs.

However, Web3 is different from Web 3.0; Web3 is a decentralized web based on distributed ledger technology. It aims to give users control over their data and identity. Web3 also focuses on empowerment and security, but Web 3.0 is a "semantic web" that aims to improve the efficiency and intelligence of the Internet. It focuses on reusing and linking machine-readable data across the web. Web 3.0 is also known as the "Linked Data Web," the "Web of Data," the "Enterprise Information Web," and the "Giant Global Graph."

If there's one word that can be used to describe Web3, it's "decentralization." Web3 utilizes distributed ledger technology to service a more decentralized Internet. In this way, users can use distributed ledger

[1] `https://www.csail.mit.edu/person/tim-berners-lee`

technology to Web3 rather than rely on centralized infrastructure and companies. In other words, users can now build and control their own identity and destiny with Web3's framework.

What Is Distributed Ledger Technology (DLT)?

Figure 1-2. *Distributed networks*

Think of it as a digital database, that is, like a financial ledger or a spreadsheet. Now, having any ledger means one can use it to store any particular information. But that doesn't mean saving it in a spreadsheet or a ledger; instead of a digital spreadsheet or application, information is stored in "blocks." Any transaction or piece of information that is stored in blocks is connected with each other to form a sequential "chain." But instead of being owned and managed by a single entity, information is decentralized and spread across multiple computers. For this reason, the most common form of DLT is the blockchain. "Blockchain" is considered to be a reliable and secure way of storing information. This is because a hacker has to manipulate every single copy of the blockchain across the entire network to access your information.

DLT's decentralized nature enables secure, transparent, and tamper-proof record-keeping. It is used in many industries, including finance, music and entertainment, diamonds and precious assets, banking, supply chain management, healthcare, insurance, and cloud services.

DLTs are used to execute CRUD (Create, Read, Update, and Delete) operations. However, blockchain is designed to be an append-only structure, meaning that users can only add more data in the form of additional blocks. Once added, data cannot be deleted or updated.

It helps store medical records and property transactions, service voting systems, supply chain management, tax collection, and so on. However, industrial experts and computer scientists have already predicted that its application will soon expand across multiple industries and applications.

Decentralization

A centralized platform refers to big tech companies holding the reins of organizations in the domains of data ownership, platform control, and taking a large chunk of the value of their product. Because of this particular model, many businesses are pushing back and seeking to gain absolute control over their data and acquire a fairer share of the value they create. For this reason, they seek platforms where there is a fairer distribution of power and control across a network. Many contemporary businesses aspire to own and control their own databases. For growth, they strive to prioritize fairness and create value for their product without relying on big tech giants. And these are some of the many dilemmas tackled by Web3.

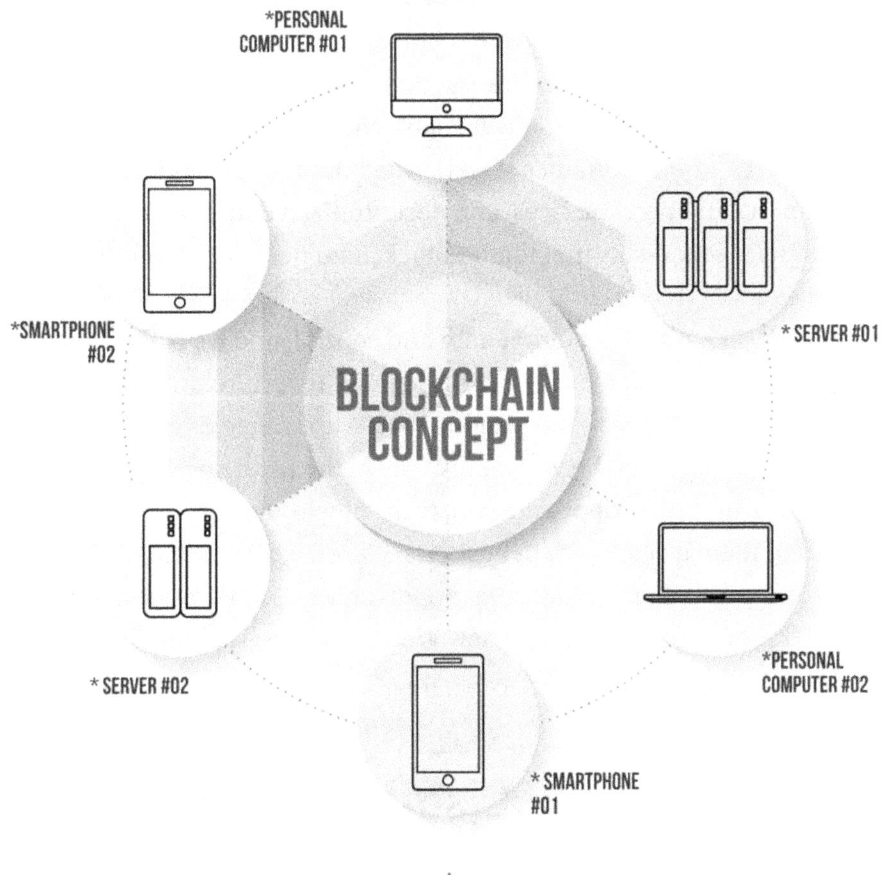

Figure 1-3. *Decentralized applications*

It's worth noticing that decentralization has been an emerging practice in the business world, even before the emergence of blockchain technology. As with Web3, there has now been a shift in paradigms from centralized to decentralized services. With Web3 now being built on decentralized protocols, the DLTs have been providing users with decentralized applications (dApps).

They have allowed users and businesses to conduct peer-to-peer transactions without the involvement of intermediaries. This disintermediation can reduce transaction costs and time consumption. There are smart contracts that will enable the construction of new business models, decentralized finance (DeFi), which is emerging as an alternative to traditional financial services, and decentralized data storage and consensus mechanisms that render blockchain networks exceptionally secure as compared to centralized databases.

With Web3, it's all about freedom and control, and we will be helping to create a roadmap for your business to join the revolution. This book will provide business leaders and professionals with strategies and insights for navigating through the Web3 universe. In the recurring chapters, we will explore in greater depth the core technologies that are empowering Web3 and their applications in business. We will cut through the various facets of blockchain to identify real opportunities. We will assess strategic considerations around building new Web3 ventures. Without further ado, let's explore these concepts more vividly.

Business Value of Distributed Ledger Technologies

When it comes to handling information, the business world is changing rapidly, and companies are lining up behind DLT systems to keep their information safe and organized. Introduced as a special way of keeping records, the history of distributed ledger technology dates back to 1976 when Diffie and Hellman crafted the concept of public-key cryptography. After that, the same mechanism further evolved from its applications in the money business into various businesses, such as retail and healthcare. Since then, organizations falling under their ambit have advocated for how DLTs have helped their businesses stay safe and work better. In fact, there has been a study that highlighted how almost every Fortune 500 enterprise and mega-corporation is trying DLT systems to keep their data safe and reliable.[2]

Figure 1-4. *Martin Hellman (left) and Whitfield Diffie (right)*

Understanding DLT for the Business World

DLT applications can potentially make the financial industry more robust, efficient, and dependable. The technology has the potential to enhance various aspects of the financial industry, such as the processing of transactions without the involvement of a third party and the processing of payments across international borders. Additionally, it has allowed the provision of financial services to the unbanked population, the area which is outside the typical reach of financial services.

[2] https://medium.com/cermati-tech/a-quick-look-into-diffie-hellman-key-exchange-24f32391b41e

DLT can also be utilized in a variety of different industries, including manufacturing, clean energy, and government financial systems. It can assist these businesses in the enhancement of their existing business processes. Due to the fact that DLT eliminates the need for a central authority, it enhances the speed at which transactions are processed, thereby lowering transaction costs per head.

Business records are stored at each network node, making it extremely difficult for an unauthorized party to manipulate or effectively attack the system. As a result, there is an effective and secure method of managing business records. DLT offers a more open and transparent method of managing records since the information can be viewed and shared across a network.

Experts cite that DLT can be exploited for a variety of purposes, including the distribution of social services, the transfer of property titles, the collection of taxes, and votes. Additionally, it may be utilized for the processing and execution of legal papers. DLT also makes it possible for individuals to make use of the technology in order to better keep and control their personal information, as well as to disclose certain bits of information when it is necessary to do so.

For Business Owners

DLT gives entrepreneurs more possibilities for internal process organization, notably in accounting and controlling, as it is always beneficial for them when several parties access the same data. These benefits rise as the network expands, which might include FC departments and partners in the same group, such as national firms and commercial partners from other organizations.

This may be done using club DLTs for a small number of participants, not public blockchains. Thus, only partners may access these ledgers. In effect, two organizations may register their partnership business transactions in a joint network in a transparent manner, eliminating the necessity for an open-books policy for sales transparency or a joint venture company to build confidence. The DLT system also allows confidence between parties who could not otherwise collaborate, including rivals. All parties can participate in joint action, including fund disposal and governance in decentralized organizations where they don't even know each other.

In Finance

DLT enables a seamless cash flow between subsidiaries at the press of a button, without the need for long delays or the involvement of several banks acting as middlemen. This is in addition to the management of separate ledgers that, in combination, improve the cash pooling process. It is also possible to implement escrow services through the use of escrow smart contracts.

There are already existing DLT systems for financing the supply chain, such as Marco Polo, which Daimler AG has previously utilized to secure payments for trade transactions. Other platforms include blockchain and Ethereum. In this particular instance, LBBW had assumed responsibility for the finance and payment promise, which enabled a normally bulky procedure of financing for international commerce to be completed in a matter of minutes.

Logistics

Evidently, Kuehne and Nagel use a decentralized ledger system to track their containers. All participants in the transport chain may read and, if needed, add to waybills (i.e., bill of lading or shipper's invoice) containing crucial cargo information like the certified container weight kept in a hyper ledger. The firm reports approximately one million monthly transactions.

A tech startup, Ubrich, has created an IT system that improves production data availability, security, and transparency. They have evidently attached data libraries to sensors in machines and production facilities to allow blockchain-encrypted production and data measurement.

To cover expenses, production capabilities can be made more flexible and plant capacity can be additionally utilized effectively. When facilities are transparently managed in a decentralized system, there are certain capabilities that can be auctioned on markets.

In Supply Chain Management

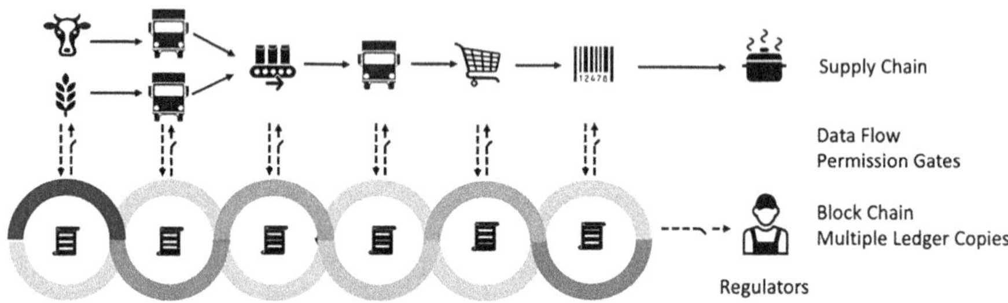

Figure 1-5. *Blockchain application in supply chain management*

In a business perspective, DLT can also be used to keep track of the whole supply chain,[3] from getting the raw materials and basic goods to making the product, selling it, and following up with customers. In addition, businesses are moving more and more toward closed recording and tracking of their own supply lines to address their own worries about their own sustainability. For example, Respeggt was set up to track chicken eggs, and Everledger's blockchain was used to make sure that "ethically clean diamonds" were real.

Healthcare

DLT can really change how healthcare works. It helps keep patient information safe and easy to share. This means doctors can see your health records when needed, but your info stays private. Plus, it helps ensure that

[3] https://www.sciencedirect.com/science/article/pii/S2211912418301408

the medicines we get are real and not fake. With DLT, patients have more say about their health data. It can also make tests and studies in hospitals clearer and more trustworthy.

Government and Public Sector

To enhance their operations and make things more transparent for everyone, governments are investigating DLT. By utilizing this technology, it is possible to develop voting systems that are more secure and cannot be altered or tampered with. In addition, it is already being utilized to maintain a transparent record of who owns the property. It can assist in the protection of personal identification documents and other documents, allowing governments to assist their residents better. When governments keep or exchange information, they may use DLT to ensure that no one alters such records without their consent.

DLT and Blockchain

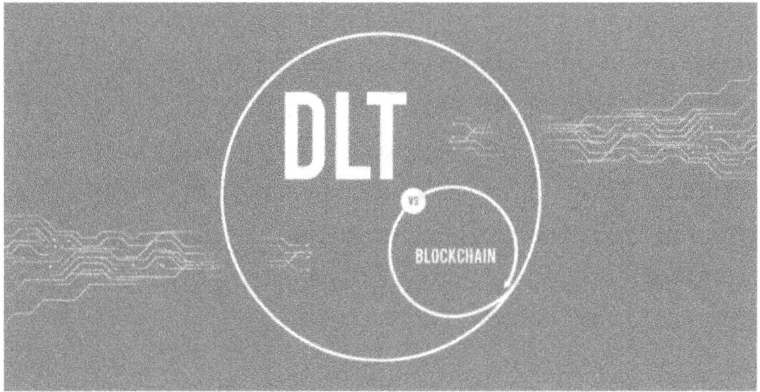

Figure 1-6. *Venn diagram for DLT*[4]

[4] https://appinventiv.com/blog/blockchain-vs-dlt-guide

Both blockchain and distributed ledger technology are widely used interchangeably in the public discourse. But the two are very distinct from one another. The use of blockchain technology makes use of a wide variety of technologies, and distributed ledger technology is one example.

Blockchain falls under the category of FTL. This technology uses encryption, making it very impossible to change. It cannot be altered and is implemented to record transactions, transfer ownership, and keep track of assets. Various sorts of transactions involving digital assets are safer, more transparent, and more trustworthy when they are conducted using blockchain technology.

In addition, blockchains are often public, which means that anybody can read the histories of transactions. Everyone has the ability to become a node in a blockchain and take part in the operations of the network. Therefore, blockchain does not require authorization.

On the other hand, different distributed ledger solutions may not always require chains of blocks in every instance. Despite this, they continue to use cryptographic validation and produce a ledger in a decentralized manner, aiming to reach a consensus among people who have a significant amount of mistrust for each other. Therefore, new information is only entered when all of the participants provide their approval for the action to be taken.

Distributed ledger technology, in contrast to blockchain, customarily imposes limitations on its accessibility, utilization, and the individuals who are authorized to serve as nodes. An additional feature is that it automatically timestamps a new entry by employing a digital signature.

Companies Using DLT

IBM

IBM leads the world in distributed ledger technology. IBM streamlines business operations with Hyperledger Fabric DLT. This improves business operations by tracking the flow of goods and their expenditure. IBM is also helping other firms adopt it and improve several sectors.

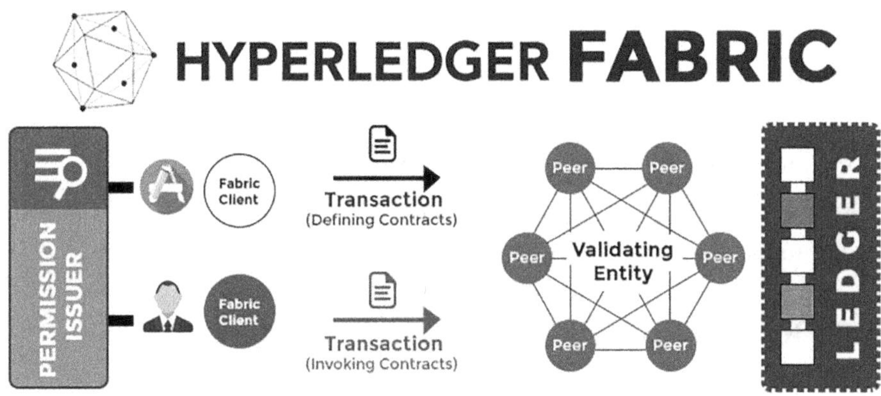

Figure 1-7. *Hyperledger Fabric transaction flow*[5]

In fact, Maersk and IBM both are using blockchain to improve their supply chain management. They're leveraging blockchain-based IoT solutions to increase platform transparency. All processes will be online and connected to the platform via IoT devices.

[5] https://www.aerowong.com/the-complete-guide-to-hyperledger-fabric-in-2023

Amazon

US-based Amazon.com has been improving its system with DLT. It shows where items originate from and streamlines their operations. Amazon continues to be a major organization implementing this system by employing this new innovation to enhance the online shopping experience.

Walmart

Walmart, which sells over $500 billion in goods, is utilizing DLT to track its items' origins and movements. This innovation helps Walmart manage stock, monitor items, and verify their authenticity. The company uses this technology to appear relevant and trustworthy. They're also guiding other retail businesses to better business practices.

Alphabet Inc. (Google)

Alphabet Inc., which controls Google, has recently shown interest in DLT, considering it a secure way to save data online. Google parent firm Alphabet believes that this technology is important for the future, and they've invested over $600 million in similar initiatives. According to Blockdata, Alphabet spends the most in DLT systems, which indicates their confidence in this new technology.

Toyota Motor Corporation

Toyota is investigating DLT to make automobiles smarter and more connected. They're employing Bitcoin-like technologies to service effective automobile communication and information management. This study is helping Toyota to lead in advanced and self-driving automobile development.

The Future

In the information technology (IT) sector, businesses are consistently searching for novel approaches to implement distributed ledger technology. It is known to assist businesses in keeping track of items in a variety of sectors, including the production of products or the management of property. They are able to function even more quickly and intelligently when they integrate DLT with other cutting-edge technologies, such as the Internet of Things (IoT) or artificial intelligence (AI). In order to develop innovative applications for this technology, there are business communities that are collaborating with one another to make it possible.

Even new enterprises are developing specialized DLT system products for a variety of company structures. As a result, it is causing a shift in the way that businesses operate all over the world. This technique is being utilized by a large corporation known as Richline Group Inc., which has ties to Warren Buffett, in order to determine the origin of jewels. In addition to this, they are collaborating with major insurance firms in China to determine the most effective ways to implement this technology.

CHAPTER 2

Strategic Overview

Distributed Ledgers and Smart Contracts

Blockchain and DLT are two words that are often used to talk about decentralized digital ledgers. People use them both a lot, but they are not the same. Blockchain is a network of computers that keep track of business deals in a shared digital ledger. A data block is used by the technology to store information. After that, different blocks join each other in a computer network to make a chain of blocks, which is where the name "blockchain" comes from.

One interesting thing about blockchain is that it has a built-in system that stops it from being changed. After records are added to the blockchain, they can't be changed or deleted by anyone else. One of the best things about blockchain is that business deals inside the network can't be changed and can't be used to commit fraud.

Blockchain is a recognized name for the technology that makes cryptocurrencies like Bitcoin work. On the other hand, companies can store information and keep track of different things. It is possible for blockchain to keep track of both physical and non-physical goods, like intellectual property or land.

When businesses collect electronic signatures, they can also use blockchain to keep track of customer information. A blockchain-based e-signature service can keep track of when, where, and what kind of gadget a client signed a file with.

G. Deshmukh and S. M. Thameem Nizamudeen, *Decentralized Business*,
https://doi.org/10.1007/979-8-8688-0953-8_2

Applications in the Business World

The idea of a blockchain was already in the works when Bitcoin was first introduced. Using digital cryptography to link together blocks of data, Satoshi Nakamoto made a record of events that can't be changed. "Satoshi Nakamoto" is a pseudonym for the person or people who introduced the concept of Bitcoin in a 2008 paper. Nakamoto remained active in creating Bitcoin and is governing blockchain until about 2010 but has not been heard from since. With digital currencies, people were stopped from duplicate and fraudulent transactions.

Figure 2-1. *Satoshi Nakamoto—unknown*[1]

The idea that led to the creation of blockchain technology is still useful today in many ways. Blockchain-based transactions might be faster and cheaper than standard ways of sending money. One great example of this is how slow and expensive foreign transactions are known to be. Even though blockchain exchanges only take minutes, moving money between accounts in the United States can take days with the current system.

[1] https://www.investopedia.com/terms/s/satoshi-nakamoto.asp

In the past few years, there have been a lot more companies that offer decentralized Bitcoin exchanges. When blockchain technology is used, transactions can be done faster and for less money. When investors use a decentralized exchange, their assets are not kept by a central authority, so they have more control and safety. The idea behind blockchain-based exchanges could be used for more traditional investments as well, even though most of them deal in cryptocurrency.

Lenders can make collateralized loans through "smart contracts" on the blockchain. When certain events happen in smart contracts set up on the blockchain, they can instantly cause a service payment, a margin call, full loan repayment, or the release of collateral. Because of this, lenders can offer better rates, and the process of getting a loan is faster and less expensive.

A lot of paperwork needs to be filled out in order to move deeds and titles to new owners and make sure that financial information is correct. Using blockchain technology to keep track of real estate deals is a safer and easier way to prove and move ownership. That could make things go more quickly, save money, and cut down on papers.

That being said, keeping private data on a public ledger (like a blockchain) might be better than using current systems that are easier to hack. Blockchain technology can be used to make identifying information safer while also making it easier for others to access in fields like healthcare, banking, education, and travel.

A next step toward using blockchain technology for voting could be putting personally identifiable information (PII) on a distributed record somewhere safe. With blockchain technology, votes can't be changed, and only people who are allowed to vote can cast them. Also, no one can vote twice. Plus, it can make voting as easy as pressing a few buttons on a phone, which may increase the number of people who vote. At the same time, the cost of running a poll would go down dramatically.

By putting patient data on a blockchain, doctors and nurses will be able to get accurate and up-to-date information. This means that people who see more than one doctor are more likely to get the best care. It might also make it faster to get medical data, which could sometimes mean faster treatment. Also, if the database has information about patients' insurance, doctors can quickly see if their care is covered.

How Is Blockchain Different from DLT?

DLT is an umbrella term used to describe many types of platforms, and blockchain is one of them. For example, the directed acyclic graph (DAG), hash graph, and holo-chain are some other types of DLT. This tells us that not every distributed ledger is a blockchain, but every blockchain is a distributed ledger.

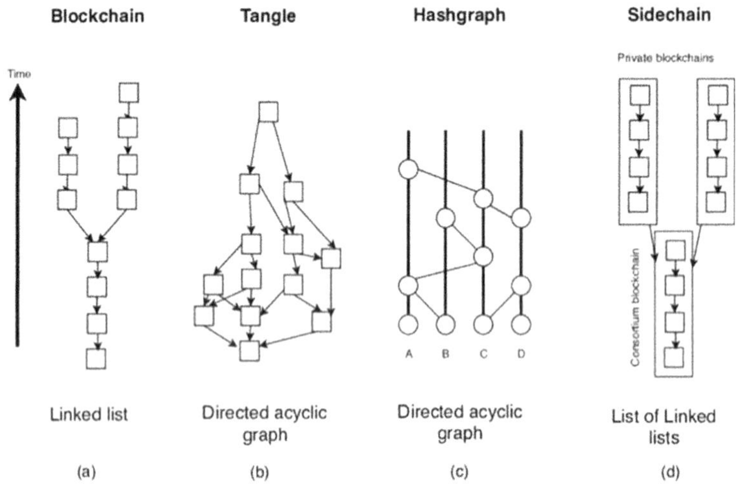

***Figure 2-2.** Existing DLT implementations*[2]

[2] https://www.researchgate.net/figure/An-overview-of-the-existing-DLTs_fig1_328475892

Blockchain is a type of data storage that works across a network of computers. It can be controlled or decentralized. In a controlled blockchain network, only one or a small group of organizations chooses who can join the network. They also dictate what rights people in the network have in the blockchain. Decentralized blockchains, on the other hand, let anyone see and confirm record processes. Bitcoin's network is a good example of this.

A lot of DLTs, like holo-chain, hash graph, and directed acyclic graph, are not controlled by a single group. Most of the time, they don't depend on one person or group to run the network.

A computer network has rules that help people agree on things. These rules help everyone work together to ensure that any new information in computer ledgers is accurate. They also ensure that all activities on the network are real, safe, and the same.

Blockchains also come in different shapes and sizes. Some can be used with permission, while others can't. Public blockchain networks, which are also known as permissionless blockchains, are open. In other words, anyone can join the network and use it. Bitcoin and Ethereum are two prominent examples.

A permission or private blockchain is a network that only its members can access. A single authority controls who can join the network, what information they can see, and what they can do. Blockchains with permissions are popular in business settings that deal with sensitive data, such as supply chain management. Whereas some DLTs, like hashgraph, don't need permission to work. This means that anyone who wants to can join in. But in general, the permissions of digital record technology, or lack thereof, depend on how it's used.

Although we only touched on the huge potential of blockchain applications in this piece, for entrepreneurs, getting ahead of the game is always a good idea, and blockchain is an effective tool to help them out. Without further ado, let's just touch on an important aspect of Blockchain and DLT, smart contracts.

Challenges Pertaining to Blockchain

Most people don't trust blockchain providers, which is the biggest problem for its wide acceptance. Corporations may have problems with the safety of the technology and the trust of people who use blockchain networks. Every activity on the blockchain is safe, private, and checked. Since the network is decentralized, there is no one in charge of making sure that transfers are valid. Consensus algorithms are what make it possible for all blockchain networks to agree on the current state of the distributed log. It makes sure that every new block adds to the one fact that all nodes in the blockchain agree on. Business leaders are more likely to trust private blockchains with no names on them.

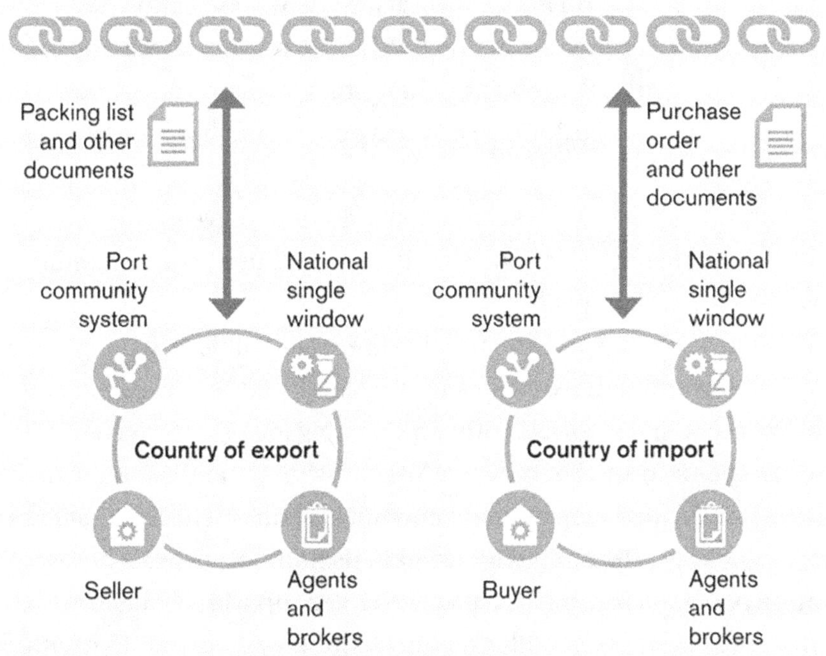

Figure 2-3. TradeLens blockchain usage[3]

However, Maersk and IBM have set up TradeLens, a global logistics network, using the IBM blockchain platform. It shows what can happen when rivals and peers work together to solve problems and gain customer trust. There are no anonymous public blockchains in TradeLens; instead, "Trust Anchors" use encrypted names. TradeLens uses a permissioned blockchain to keep shipping documents safe, private, and easy to track.

[3] https://mag.wcoomd.org/magazine/wco-news-87/tradelens/

The technical ability to grow may stop people from using blockchain, especially for public blockchains. There are thousands of deals that can be done every second on legacy transaction networks. Almost 2,000 purchases happen every second with Visa. The two most well-known blockchain networks, Bitcoin and Ethereum, have slow transaction speeds. Bitcoin can only handle 3–7 transactions per second, but Ethereum can handle 20.

Meanwhile, private blockchain networks don't have to worry about being able to grow because their nodes are designed to handle transactions in a safe space.

But it will soon be possible to solve the scale problem in interesting ways. The Lightning Network speeds up deals by adding a second layer to the blockchain network. Another interesting idea is sharding, which divides nodes into smaller network "orchards" that handle their own activities. Third, bad management and unclear rules. The fact that laws aren't completely clear about blockchain technology makes it harder for more people to use it. Laws have never kept up with changes in technology. This is true for blockchain technology. One problem with blockchain (and its original goal) is that it makes review less possible.

A lot of businesses use blockchain to do business. There aren't any clear rules. There is no protection because no one follows the rules for blockchain. Smart contracts are one example of an industry that needs rules. Without smart contract rules, blockchain adoption and funding would go down.

Individual shocks could affect decentralized networks if they are not properly thought out. There is a good case for blockchain applications to work with the regulatory processes that are already in place. The government and other businesses with strict rules may be able to solve these problems with blockchain law. However, people in charge of all kinds of businesses need to know how technology affects businesses and customers.

Another big problem is that blockchain networks don't work with each other. A lot of projects use their own blockchain platforms and solutions, each with their own rules, programming languages, ways of reaching agreement, and safety steps for privacy.

Blockchain is in a "state of disorder" because there aren't any shared standards that let networks talk to each other. Inconsistencies in the blockchain system make it less secure, which makes widespread use almost impossible.

However, setting industry-wide guidelines for many blockchain protocols could help businesses work together on app development, test proofs of concept, share blockchain solutions, and make it easier for new systems to connect to existing ones. Ark is one project that lets different blockchains work together and communicate and send money between them. The Inter Blockchain Communication (IBC) protocol lets blockchain economies like Cosmos share information and work together instead of separately.

Another problem for businesses is combining Bitcoin with old systems. For most businesses to adopt blockchain, they will need to either rework their current system or come up with a way to combine the two technologies. Companies don't have enough blockchain experts to take part in this process because there aren't enough developers. Help from a third party can solve this problem. It takes a lot of time and money to adapt to most market options. Most businesses don't use blockchain because there is a high chance of data loss and hacking. Every company is afraid to change its database because there is a good chance that data will be lost or damaged.

Nevertheless, older systems can now connect to blockchain backends thanks to new technologies. The Modex Blockchain Database lets people who aren't tech-savvy use blockchain technology without having to worry about losing their info.

Smart Contracts

In 1994, Nick Szabo, a legal scholar and computer scientist, came up with the idea of a computer protocol that would not only set the terms of a trade but also carry it out. Usually, traditional contracts need lawyers or the government to carry out the exchange that was agreed upon. He came up with an idea of a type of contract that could carry out and enforce themself. Szabo said that these contracts would be like a cash machine. For instance, let's say you want to go to the store and buy a candy bar. In order to do that, you have to follow the normal steps: pay the price, and the shop will give you the candy bar. This conversation doesn't just happen, of course. There needs to be a cashier to carry out the deal and a legal body to make sure it is followed. For example, if the teller breaks the contract by taking your money but not giving you the candy bar, the contract may need to be enforced by police or lawyers. However, if we talk about vending machines, they handle every part of a deal on their own. To buy a candy bar from a vending machine, you have to pick out what you want and put money into the machine. The machine checks your payment, completes the deal, and then you get your candy bar right away. There is no need for a checker, a lawyer, or the government as long as the vending machine is safe. The deal is atomic, which means it should always go smoothly or not at all.

Figure 2-4. *Nick Szabo—computer scientist*[4]

What Are Smart Contracts?

Smart contracts carry out a deal without the need for middlemen—just like vending machines. People who want to do business with each other only need to agree on the terms and put a cryptocurrency coin into the program. The smart contract will then carry out the desired digital trade.

Smart Contracts spell out and record the terms of the deal, including what each party needs to do. Let's say you give the cashier a dollar. The cashier has to give you the candy bar. The only goal of a standard contract is to spell out these terms.

A normal contract by itself can't make someone follow the rules it sets out. As an alternative, a legal or government third party watches the execution of a standard contract, making sure that each party keeps their end of the deal. If the terms are broken, the parties must rely on the third party to make things right.

[4] https://www.bitcoinerbooks.com/people/nick-szabo

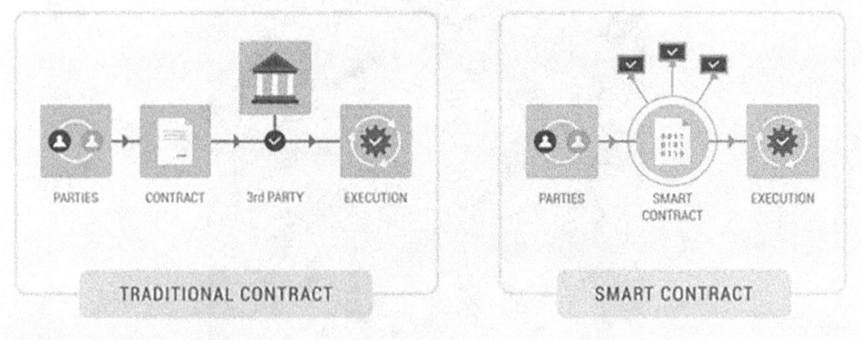

Figure 2-5. *Traditional contract vs. smart contract*[5]

However, new developments in distributed ledger technology mean that contracts don't need to be overseen by lawyers or other middlemen. For the first time, smart contracts let people carry out and maintain agreements without the need for middlemen.

One good thing about smart contracts is that they are independent. When there aren't any agents involved, there's no need to pay them. The costs of big deals could go down significantly because of this. In addition, smart contracts don't need to be checked by third parties in order to be carried out correctly and on time. Because of this, smart contracts might be safer, faster, and cheaper than normal contracts.

Another thing is that smart contracts have the same amount of security and openness as the distributed ledger they work on. An open ledger lets everyone in the network see every activity that takes place on it. Because everything is clear, you can check your deal and feel safe knowing that it was done correctly. Additionally, the records of your transaction are not easily changed or deleted on a distributed log. If they are changed or deleted, you will be made aware of the change. Smart contracts and public ledgers both have benefits that can't be found anywhere else, such as better security and openness.

[5] https://www.cryptoninjas.net/what-are-smart-contracts/

Lastly, smart contracts make deals easier than was hard to do before. Even though smart contracts can be used for simple transactions, they can also be used to define and carry out complicated talks with many parties within a certain amount of time. They can be used over and over again after they have been made. Another thing that can be done is to use multiple smart contracts together to make deals even more complicated.

The Regulatory Challenges of Blockchain and Smart Contracts

People in the media, companies, and governments have been very interested in the pros and cons of distributed ledger technology (DLTs) over the past few years. Distributed ledger technologies are still pretty new, but they have the ability to completely change the way society and the economy work. Because of these big changes, governments are having to deal with a lot of tough problems. They are trying to find a balance between encouraging new ideas and protecting customers from the bad effects that might happen by accident.

In particular, it shows how important it is to get help and follow the right rules in order to lower the legal uncertainty and risks that come from smart contracts that use distributed ledger technology (DLT). This also shows that efforts to work together internationally often play a big part in fixing problems with territory that come up because of smart contracts.

With the rise of smart contracts, there are also regulatory issues that need to be dealt with by states. There is a lot of legal confusion about smart contracts because they are new. And when it comes to clearing things up, governments have to give advice and make the necessary rules.

Figure 2-6. *EU Blockchain Forum*[6]

DLT-based smart contracts are in danger. Regulatory systems need to be able to deal with these risks while also encouraging new ideas. International cooperation is a must if we want to solve the problems that smart contracts cause with authority. The fact that existing regulatory systems are broken up across jurisdictions shows how complicated the problems are. Different countries have put in place different kinds of rules.

A study on the laws and rules that apply to blockchains and smart contracts has been put together by the Blockchain Observatory and Forum of the European Union. There are policies in place in some US states, but the federal government is still only partially supporting them.

Smart contracts can work because they use public blockchains, which anyone can look at. People who weren't meant to be able to see personal or business information that is included in smart contracts may be able to do so. Privacy concerns must be taken care of by regulators, and transparency must be kept.

---

[6] https://www.eublockchainforum.eu/news/eubof-conference-blockchain-key-enabler-innovation-europe-and-world-8th-july-brussels

Since blockchain technology can't be changed, you can't make any changes to a smart contract once it's been built and used. But this makes things more difficult if something goes wrong. This makes it harder to fix a bug or deal with an effect that you don't want. Finding a balance between what can't be changed and what can be done is the judicial problem.

In a nutshell, governments have to find a way to balance new technologies with protecting consumers. This is not easy because blockchain technology and smart contracts are growing so quickly. In order to effectively handle this disruptive technology, there must be full regulatory guidelines and cooperation between countries.

In conclusion, blockchain technology and smart contracts offer businesses a glimpse into a future of secure, transparent, and efficient transactions. While the technology is still in development, it holds immense potential to streamline processes, reduce costs, and nurture trust in a digital age. Whether automating supply chains, managing intellectual property, or facilitating secure payments, blockchain and smart contracts are poised to revolutionize the way businesses operate.

CHAPTER 3

DLT for Cloud Professionals

Cloud computing has become very popular in this modern age. You don't need to own or maintain any computer resources, like servers or storage, to access and use them; all you need is an Internet connection. Here, you may effortlessly get what you need, use it for as long as you need it, and then put it back. This technology features on-demand self-service, ubiquitous access via a wide network, resource pooling for greater efficiency, and measured services.

Companies like Amazon, Google, and Microsoft are at the forefront of the cloud computing industry. They all work essentially the same way: you upload information to their servers and then access it online. Dependence on these centralized systems, however, does not come without its share of problems.

They are vulnerable to disruptions, like the one that happened in 2020 when Google services were down, leaving many people without access to Gmail and YouTube. You should occasionally expect less than optimal performance from their servers, especially if they are situated far from your location.

It can also be quite costly to ensure their security and conduct routine maintenance on them. Privacy and security on the servers are issues, especially in the case of a data breach.

G. Deshmukh and S. M. Thameem Nizamudeen, *Decentralized Business*,
https://doi.org/10.1007/979-8-8688-0953-8_3

One possible solution to these problems is to apply DLT and AI to decentralize these services. It is necessary to spread things out further to reduce the likelihood that everything will occur simultaneously. Even more so, it adds safeguards that make it harder for unauthorized parties to alter your data.

The traditional, centralized cloud architecture is undergoing a period of change because of problems like latency, bandwidth limits, and the need to handle data in real time. New, high-performance computer solutions are always needed. With the rise of decentralized cloud computing, we are entering the age of edge intelligence. This is a big change because it moves computing power closer to the edges of the network.

What Is Decentralized Cloud Computing?

Decentralized cloud computing, which utilizes DLT, is a service that is quickly becoming an important component of the routine operations of businesses and organizations. It offers a network of peer-to-peer cloud marketplaces. Cloud services are offered to customers who join this network, and users may also rent out their unused computing, networking, storage, and other resources to other users. Decentralized infrastructure is in charge of controlling the spread and host location of cloud services in cloud computing.

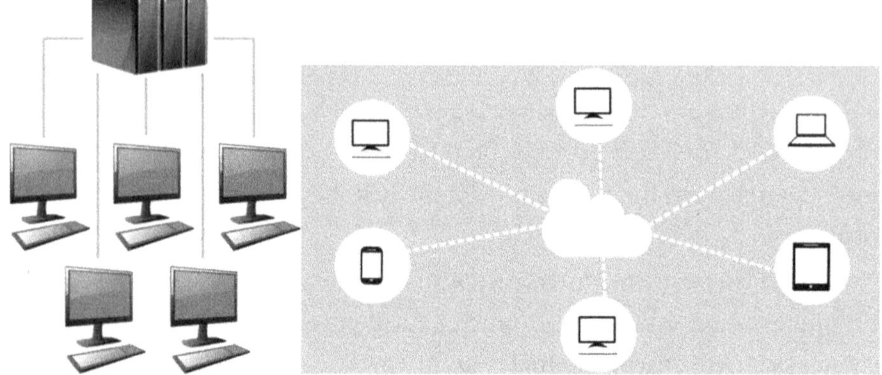

Figure 3-1. *Traditional vs. decentralized computing*

With decentralization, you don't need a single server or data center. On the other hand, all of the linked gadgets use the same process to make decisions. Computer resources are moved closer to end users' devices, like their computers or phones. This is what the word "decentralized cloud" means. In an ideal decentralized cloud design, every node on the network could function as a small server. With these devices, you don't need a big central server to work together, stream video, or share files.

Why Not Centralized Cloud Computing?

Centralized cloud computing service companies charge for their services. While bigger organizations may not be too affected by these taxes, smaller businesses may feel their effects much more acutely. Amazon Web Services (AWS), a major cloud provider, charges approximately $23 per month for the storage space available in its cloud data centers. However, businesses can still utilize data analytics to review their data and improve their services and goods, even when they say they do not use user data unethically.

Some cloud storage providers may also use the data saved on their servers to send targeted adverts to the data owner, which is something that many companies find intrusive. Worse yet, cloud platforms increasingly employ a server model with a single point of failure, greatly increasing the chance of data compromise.

Objectives of Decentralized Cloud Computing

No Monopolized Control

A decentralized network ensures that no one person or group can completely control the site. For this reason, the site shouldn't be run by just one group. Monopolies are discouraged, and fair competition is kept up.

Enhanced Competition

The decentralized setup of the network should encourage these businesses to compete in a healthy way. There will be enhanced service, especially in data storage and related areas, because there will be more competition.

Protection of Users' Privacy

One important part of user data control is the right to delete data and the guarantee that it will be returned to its original form when retrieved from the service provider. These rights should never be taken away. To protect users' privacy even more, only the users should be able to see their info.

Reliability

By building redundancy into the system, the data should be kept safe from being lost or changed. It's also important to be reliable. Reliability is a big part of keeping users' trust in the service.

Affordability

Customers should be able to afford the service because it doesn't have steep prices associated with centralized cloud services.

Quality Services

It would be effective to give service providers and users reasons to join the network. Getting great services at fair prices or getting paid for resources are two examples of things that could be thought of as rewards.

Storage and Power-Sharing

People who have the extra processing power or storage space can rent them out to other people for a fee in a decentralized cloud storage system. Users of the global network who access these tools after they are found will be charged for the services they use.

Enhanced Security

The data is safer because the network is not centralized, which gets rid of the system's possible weak spot. Strong systems ensure that people pay for services, which in turn awards good service providers and holds bad service providers responsible.

According to the platform's makers, Ethernity Cloud by Ethereum can now run smart contracts and decentralized apps. In this case, instead of depending on a centralized authority made up of cloud service providers, the Ethereum cloud will utilize smart contracts. If you want your next project to work, you need to hire competent developers.

One category of decentralized cloud computing that is currently dominating the market is decentralized cloud data storage. Storj and Siacoin are two service providers who have made a name for themselves in the industry by giving security that server-client cloud companies can't match.

There is no doubt that new service providers will join the business as it continues to flourish. Startups such as Filecoin and MaidSafe are already utilizing cutting-edge methods in an effort to carve out a share of the market for cloud data storage for themselves.

Application of DLT in Cloud Computing

Decentralized cloud computing enables safe data sharing, efficient resource allocation, and decentralized application hosting. Facilitating electronic data storage with features like smart contracts, immutable storage, and decentralized identity management creates an environment that is both transparent and free of trust.

Supply Chain Management

Decentralized technological solutions enable secure, transparent, and immutable supply chain management. Reducing fraud, improving accountability, and streamlining transactions are all made feasible by being able to trace transactions from start to end. Decentralized solutions can cut down on counterfeiting, which is a bonus on top of improving customer trust and making inventory management easier.

Managing User IDs and Permissions

Decentralized technology eliminates the need for a governing body to manage user identities and access permissions. Advantages of this approach include providing fast, secure, and transparent identity verification; reducing the frequency and severity of data breaches; and eliminating middlemen. Users now have more say over their personal information and data.

Data Management and Storage

Using decentralized technologies can make data management and storage more secure. It eliminates the need for middlemen, making effective data sharing easier, and reduces the frequency of data breaches. It ensures the data's immutability and integrity, boosts transparency, and reduces costs.

Financial Transaction Processing and Payment Processing

DLT allows for secure, transparent, and efficient financial transactions and payment processing. It also facilitates P2P transfers, eliminates middlemen, and reduces transaction costs.

Advantages of Decentralized Cloud Computing

Enhanced Security

Decentralized cloud computing offers a higher degree of security than centralized cloud computing by utilizing cryptographic ideas and dispersing data over multiple nodes.

Data Ownership and Control

Users can effectively align themselves with decentralization principles since they have more control over their data, including the power to define access rights and usage restrictions.

Cost-Effectiveness

Since decentralized cloud computing does away with the need for centralized data centers, it saves infrastructure expenses.

Scalability

Unlike traditional systems, the decentralized paradigm allows for dynamic changes to resource demands, leading to enhanced scalability.

Real-World Examples of Decentralized Cloud Computing

Because AIGC, Web3, and the Metaverse are growing so quickly, the need for cheap computer power is growing at an exponential rate. There are now a lot of new projects working on building an open cloud network to make the most of these unused computer resources, especially for AI in the business world. We'll talk about a few of the most notable projects going on right now.

Figure 3-2. *LogCortex Labs*[1]

It is a peer-to-peer, decentralized, and open-source DLT network. It can easily combine AI models. Now, people who make AI models can put them on the DLT and use them in smart contracts. Cortex is known for putting the first AI on the DLT and making it possible for AI to make decisions while processes are happening on the DLT. It is cutting-edge DLT because it can use AI and ML. Using on-chain inference lets independent applications reach the goals of smart contracts when it is put into action.

[1] https://cortexlabs.ai/

Bittensor

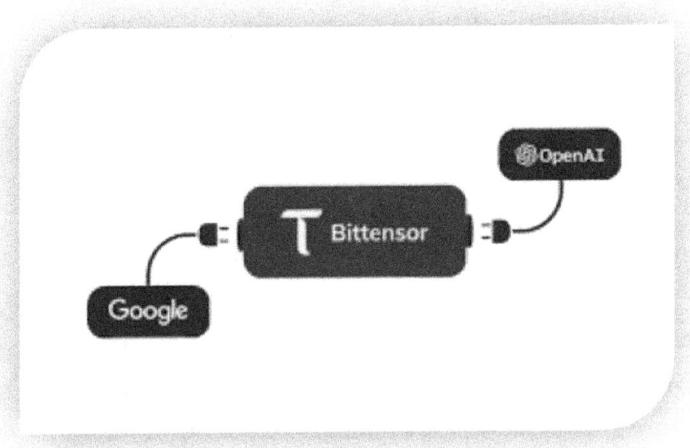

Figure 3-3. *Role of Bittensor as DLT*[2]

A decentralized machine learning network built on DLT is run by the open-source system Bittensor. People can access a global network of machine learning models that can't be censored. This method is a lot like the Bitcoin mining network in a lot of ways. In order to make it easier for sellers and buyers of AI models to trade data in an open and honest way, Bittensor wants to get these models in their own market. It's different from other companies in the same field because it encourages AI models to be involved and focuses on making markets that create value.

[2] https://bittensor.com

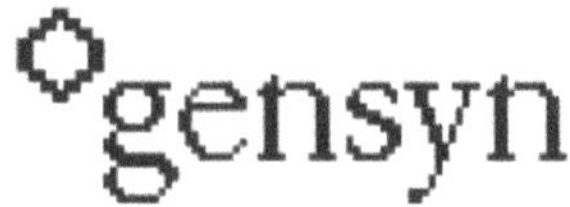

Figure 3-4. *Logo for Gensyn*[3]

Gensyn

The goal of the Gensyn machine learning computing network is to create an open-access global supercluster with all of the world's computing capabilities. The program makes good use of empty computer resources by letting developers train deep learning models across a network of linked devices. The network uses DLT application technology to make sure that learning tasks are finished and to start token-based payouts. Gensyn's goal is to make computing power more accessible by using decentralized technologies. This will give AI developers an option that is better for the environment, can be scaled up, and doesn't cost as much.

[3] https://www.gensyn.ai/

CHAPTER 4

Use Cases of DLTs in Cloud Computing

You can easily run blockchain networks on cloud computing platforms and services because they have all the infrastructure you need. Because of the nature of cloud computing being flexible, blockchain networks can change their size based on demand, which makes good use of resources. By utilizing cloud computing, organizations have the option to establish a decentralized network with blockchain technology while simultaneously benefiting from scalability, fault tolerance, security, and cost efficiency. The utilization of blockchain technology in conjunction with cloud computing enables the development of robust, decentralized apps that provide businesses with enhanced control over their data and computational assets.

DLT Use Cases for Cloud Computing

DLT has the potential to revolutionize cloud computing by providing safe, transparent, and decentralized solutions for various applications. Blockchain is well-suited for cloud computing as it enables the creation of immutable transactions and data records. This section will explore several applications of distributed ledger technology in cloud computing.

G. Deshmukh and S. M. Thameem Nizamudeen, *Decentralized Business*,
https://doi.org/10.1007/979-8-8688-0953-8_4

Secure Data Storage

DLT offers secure data storage alternatives for cloud computing. It utilizes cryptography to securely store data, restricting access to certain keys and cryptographic signatures. Once the data is stored, it can become immutable, and the ledger is regulated by rules. Because all copies stored across the network must be targeted simultaneously for an attack to succeed, DLT is less vulnerable to cybercrime.

Each node in the distributed ledger technology network maintains its own version of the ledger, and any changes made are propagated throughout the whole network. Transactions are completed, encrypted, and serve as a foundation for further transactions if the network can agree on the validity of the latest ledger.

Smart Contracts

Smart contracts can execute tasks once specific conditions are met by establishing the rules and requirements that need to be fulfilled. Examples of these tasks include the disbursement of payments, the recording of assets, and the issuance of notifications. Smart contracts eliminate manual processes and intermediaries to improve operations, reduce costs, and prevent conflicts. This removes the necessity for intermediaries. They are ideal for many applications that leverage cloud computing, including supply chain management, decentralized apps, and financial services. Cloud computing could enhance its efficiency, security, and transparency through improved utilization of smart contracts.

Supply Chain Management

DLT can provide real-time tracking and visibility of commodities along the supply chain by creating a secure, transparent, and tamper-proof record of transactions and data. It can utilize smart contracts to automate operations and reduce the necessity for manual intervention. This leads to improved efficiency and a decrease in mistakes. DLT can help prevent fraud and ensure compliance by recording every transaction on the ledger. Distributed ledger technology also has the ability to enhance communication and decrease conflicts among many parties in the supply chain. It has the potential to enhance supply chain management by providing a secure, transparent, and efficient mechanism for tracking and managing products in the cloud.

Identity Verification

Users can manage their personal information and reduce the risk of identity theft by utilizing distributed ledger technology, which establishes a secure and decentralized system for managing digital identities. DLT can ensure the secrecy and security of personal data by employing encryption, allowing users to disclose only necessary information for specific transactions. It can enable instant verification of identities, reducing the reliance on human intervention and intermediaries. Streamlining workflows can decrease expenses and minimize errors. This technology can create a tamper-proof log of transactions, enabling audits and compliance verifications, and has the potential to enhance identity verification by providing a secure, transparent, and efficient mechanism for managing digital identities in the cloud.

Decentralized Applications (dApps)

Decentralized applications (dApps) are software programs that function on a peer-to-peer network or blockchain instead of a single computer or centralized server. dApps are controlled by their users as a group, allowing for secure, transparent, and decentralized operations. They can be used for various purposes like gaming, banking, and social networking, offering benefits such as reduced costs, increased efficiency, and improved security. Cloud computing can provide more democratic, trustworthy, and accessible services to users through the usage of dApps. Users can access these services from any location and maintain transparent transaction records. Users should be cautious and conduct thorough investigation before engaging with decentralized applications due to their decentralized nature, which can hinder the ability to identify or hold accountable individuals involved in criminal activities.

Tokenization

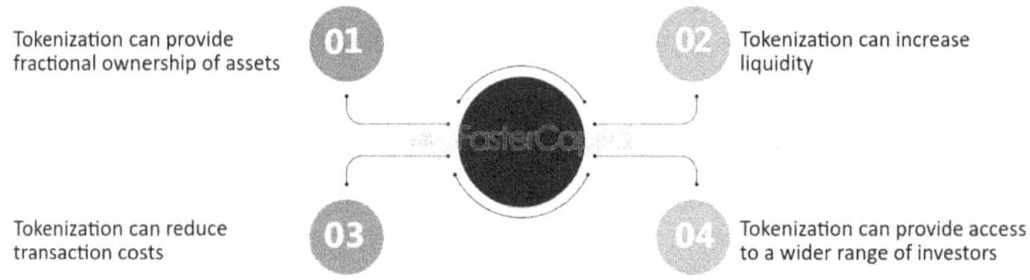

Figure 4-1. *Advantages of tokenization*[1]

Tokenization in distributed ledger technology for cloud computing involves converting data into unique, immutable, and traceable units called tokens. Encrypting tokens and recording their ownership and transfer on a distributed ledger enhance data security, privacy, and integrity. Tokens can be transferred over a distributed ledger. Tokenization enables the creation of digital assets, like tokens representing real-world assets, for trading on decentralized networks. Smart contracts enable tokenization to automate and simplify complex tasks such as managing supply chains, verifying identities, and executing financial transactions.

[1] https://fastercapital.com/content/Tokenization--Transforming-Assets-with-Distributed-Ledger-Technology.html#Benefits-of-Tokenization-using-DLT

Voting Systems

DLT enables real-time tracking and verification of votes by creating a secure, transparent, and tamper-proof record of transactions and data. It can utilize encryption to safeguard the privacy and security of voting data. This allows voters to vote without the possibility of being influenced or deceived. Remote voting is a use case of distributed ledger technology that can decrease the necessity for physical polling locations and enhance accessibility. Utilizing DLT can also simplify audits and compliance checks to enhance the integrity of the voting process.

Healthcare

DLT offers the capability to enable immediate tracking and authentication of patient data, medical imaging, research, and other associated fields. It can ensure the confidentiality and security of healthcare data through encryption. This allows patients and healthcare professionals to exchange and access crucial information without the possibility of being deceived or defrauded. Distributed ledger technology can also simplify audits and compliance checks, hence ensuring the integrity of healthcare systems. Users would be able to create digital assets like tokens representing healthcare services or medical information that can be traded on decentralized platforms.

Financial Services

Not only DLT offers secure, transparent, and immutable records of transactions and data, but also allows for instant tracking and validation of financial transactions. Distributed ledger technology can ensure the secrecy and security of financial data through the use of encryption. Individuals and financial organizations can exchange and access crucial information securely, without the threat of manipulation or fraud. DLT can also create digital assets like tokens representing financial instruments for trading on decentralized marketplaces.

Internet of Things (IoT)

Cryptography can safeguard the privacy and security of data gathered by the Internet of Things (IoT) through distributed ledger technology. This allows devices to interact and access information securely without the threat of manipulation or fraud. DLT can provide edge computing, reducing the need for centralized processing and improving the speed and efficiency of IoT systems. DLT can facilitate audits and compliance checks, hence enhancing the reliability of Internet of Things systems.

Real-World Implementations

Decentralized storage solutions are becoming more disruptive as cloud computing evolves. It utilizes a dispersed network of individual storage nodes, as opposed to centralized data centers used by typical cloud storage providers. This peer-to-peer strategy has numerous benefits and has the potential to revolutionize data storage and retrieval on the cloud.

The economic benefit of decentralized storage is a key advantage of this storage architecture. Traditional cloud storage providers incur significant expenses due to the infrastructure and operation of large data centers. Moreover, these expenses are often included in user fees, leading to storage options that could be costly. Decentralized storage disrupts this paradigm by utilizing a dispersed network of individual contributors. By renting out their vacant storage space, contributors enable users to store data at a significantly reduced cost compared to centralized providers. This leads to a more competitive market, lowering storage costs for users and ensuring a steady revenue for storage providers.

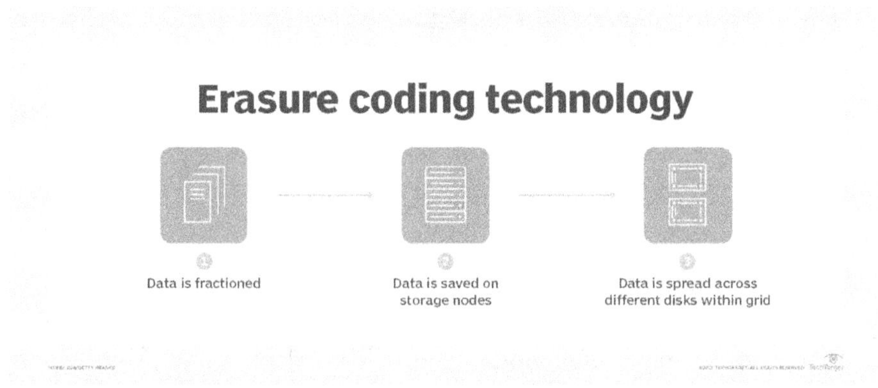

Figure 4-2. *Distributed storage workflow*[2]

Utilizing decentralized storage is a significant advancement in safeguarding and securing data. Centralized data centers are susceptible to cybercriminals and government meddling due to being a single point of vulnerability. Decentralized storage minimizes risk by distributing data throughout a wide network of independent nodes. Malevolent actors' capacity to access a comprehensive dataset is greatly hindered, if not made impossible, by this.

Decentralized storage solutions often utilize cryptographic proofs and smart contracts that rely on blockchain technology. These technologies assure data integrity and accountability by allowing users to verify the secure storage of their data and the compliance of storage providers with specified terms. Information is often secured using encryption and safeguarded utilizing replication or erasure coding. Furthermore, data is consistently protected. Replication is the act of storing duplicates of data across many nodes. This guarantees data accessibility in case of node failures. Erasure coding is a technique that involves breaking down data into tiny fragments and distributing them across a network. The remaining bits can be used to reconstruct the original data, even if some fragments are missing, providing a barricade against data loss due to node failures.

[2] https://www.techtarget.com/searchstorage/definition/erasure-coding#

The inherent robustness of decentralized storage against single points of failure is a key advantage of this storage method. Implementing typical centralized storage solutions necessitates a single data center. In the event of a power outage or hardware malfunction at this data center, all stored data will be inaccessible. Decentralized storage reduces the risk described by distributing data across a geographically dispersed network. Even if one or more nodes encounter issues, the data can still be readily accessed from the nodes that remain functional across the network. A single bad actor compromising a single node inside the network will not significantly impact the overall data security of the network. The data can still be retrieved and accessed from other nodes that have copies or parts of it.

The decentralized storage landscape is always changing and dynamic. Filecoin, Sia, and Storj are innovative solutions that are making a big influence on the industry with their inventive approaches. These platforms offer user-friendly interfaces and robust security features, making them attractive alternatives to traditional cloud storage options. Furthermore, a constant stream of inventive solutions is exacerbating the challenges of decentralization and security. This establishes a competitive environment that benefits users by lowering costs, enhancing security measures, and offering a broader range of storage options.

A significant change in cloud computing has occurred due to the development of decentralized storage solutions. These solutions offer a data storage technique that is public, decentralized, and secure. They achieve this by using a distributed network of storage nodes. People and businesses seeking a dependable and economical way to store their data may find decentralized storage attractive because of its cost-effectiveness, enhanced security features, and resilience against single points of failure. As decentralized storage systems evolve, we may expect the introduction of advanced technologies that will transform how we engage with cloud-stored data.

Decentralized storage systems offer a convincing alternative to traditional cloud storage providers. The solutions provide enhanced security, cost-effectiveness, and resistance to single points of failure. They achieve this by dispersing data throughout a network of autonomous nodes. The decentralized storage sector is growing, leading to the development of innovative solutions that will revolutionize data storage and access in the cloud.

CHAPTER 5

Integrating DLTs in Cloud-Based Infrastructures

Today's organizations are seeking to develop new solutions to enhance the security, transparency, and accessibility of their cloud-based infrastructure. Integrating distributed ledger technology with cloud-based infrastructure can bring significant advantages to organizations but involves a complex process that requires meticulous planning, design, and execution. The process commences with choosing the suitable DLT platform, and one must possess a thorough understanding of distributed ledger technology and cloud computing technologies, including their unique features, capabilities, and compromises.

This chapter provides a thorough and practical approach to incorporating distributed ledger technology into cloud-based infrastructure. By following the step-by-step strategy outlined in this tutorial, organizations can effectively leverage the advantages of DLT to enhance the security and transparency of their internal infrastructure.

G. Deshmukh and S. M. Thameem Nizamudeen, *Decentralized Business*,
https://doi.org/10.1007/979-8-8688-0953-8_5

Identifying the Use Case

As discussed in the previous chapter, organizations have to determine the specific business process or function where DLT can provide the most value. This step aims to ensure that the integration aligns with the firm's strategic objectives and provides benefits that meet specific business needs. If the integration lacks a clear use case, it may lead to unnecessary expenses, complexity, and hazards without providing any significant value.

Various use cases have specific requirements and limitations that can influence the selection of the appropriate DLT platform, network design, smart contract development, and other integration factors. Organizations can focus their efforts and resources on the most promising areas by defining the use case.

Ensuring a seamless integration of distributed ledger technology into their cloud infrastructure is crucial for making a significant impact. It is crucial to dedicate ample time and effort to identify the use case; it could be accomplished by engaging the key stakeholders and conducting thorough analysis and research to ensure a thorough understanding of the business's needs, opportunities, and challenges.

Choosing the Right DLT Platform

The DLT platform of your organization will be the foundation of the entire system, and the integration's result will be greatly affected by the platform's features, capabilities, and limitations. An ideal distributed ledger technology platform should align with the organization's use case, technical needs, and strategic objectives. The platform should have the required competency to handle smart contracts and other distributed ledger technology services, while also ensuring security, scalability, and interoperability.

The distributed ledger technology platform should be interoperable with the existing cloud infrastructure and tools to enable smooth integration and operation. The community, ecosystem, and support of the platform should be considered since they can impact the integration's success and the company's ability to maintain and improve the system.

Organizations should select a suitable DLT platform based on their requirements. Popular platforms include Ethereum, Hyperledger Fabric, Corda, and Quorum. Each platform has its unique features, capabilities, and trade-offs, so choose the one that aligns best with your use case.

Ethereum (ETH)

Ethereum utilizes the JSON-RPC (remote procedure call) Application Programming Interface to communicate with other systems. Users can utilize the Application Programming Interface (API) to submit transactions, manage accounts, and check the current status of the blockchain. Developers can construct decentralized applications that operate directly on the blockchain using Ethereum's smart contract technology.

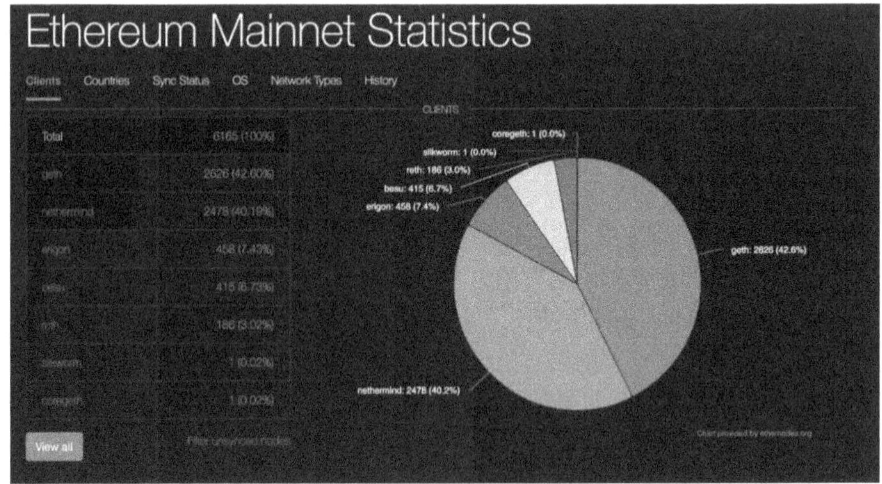

Figure 5-1. *Client diversity and distribution on Ethereum*[1]

The Ethereum Light Client Protocol (ELCP) enables the downloading of a limited amount of data from the Ethereum blockchain in an efficient and safe manner. Therefore, it is easy to integrate with the existing cloud infrastructure by using scaling options. Conversely, limitations in scalability can have a detrimental effect on performance in corporate environments.

[1] https://ethernodes.org/

Hyperledger Fabric

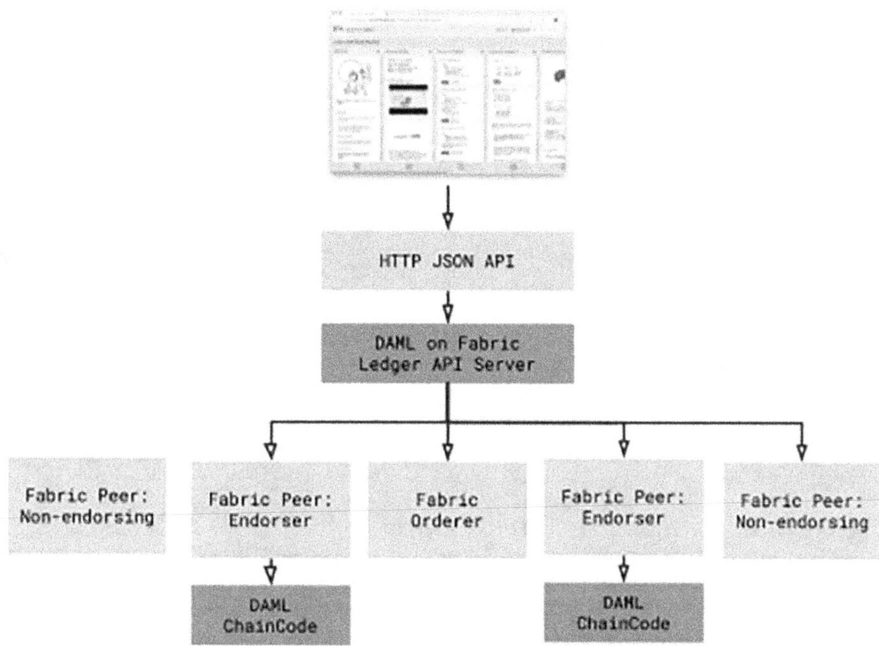

Figure 5-2. *Workflow for dApps on Hyperledger Fabric*[2]

Hyperledger Fabric provides a platform-specific REST API for application programming. The API facilitates apps to interact with the blockchain through HTTP requests. Docker containers and Software Development Kits (SDKs) enable seamless integration with cloud systems. This requires more programming effort than Ethereum but offers a high level of flexibility and customization. Fabric Software Development Kits (SDKs) provide advanced abstractions for constructing client applications. Hyperledger Fabric also includes features that allow it to communicate with other DLT systems, facilitating smooth communication between different DLT networks.

[2] https://www.hyperledger.org/blog/2020/04/02/running-productivity-apps-on-hyperledger-fabric

Corda

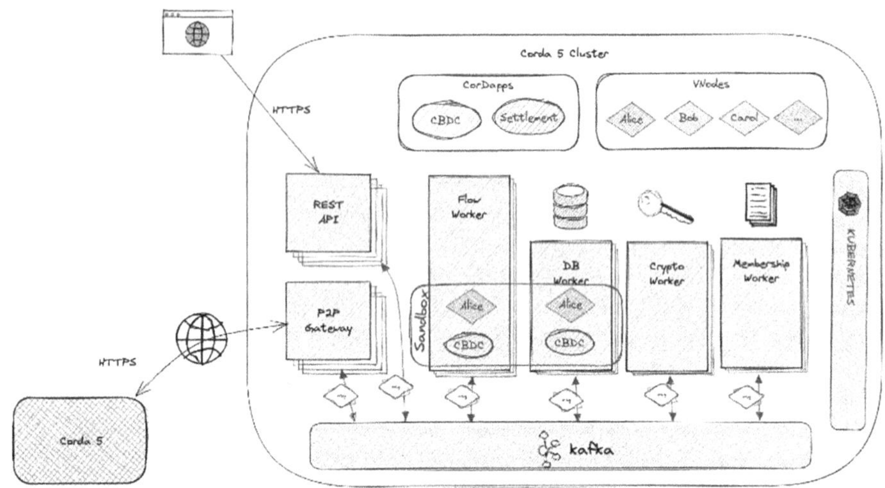

Figure 5-3. *Corda cluster architecture*[3]

Corda provides an HTTP-based API to enhance collaboration with other financial systems. It was designed primarily for cloud deployments and is interoperable with major cloud providers. The nodes of the platform can be configured to establish connections with other systems, including RESTful web services, databases, and other systems inside the Corda network. Corda's states and transactions approach enables secure and efficient interaction with the blockchain. This expedited method is suitable for enterprise use cases; however, participation is limited to approved members.

[3] https://docs.r3.com/en/platform/corda/5.2/key-concepts/cordapp-dev/building.html

Quorum

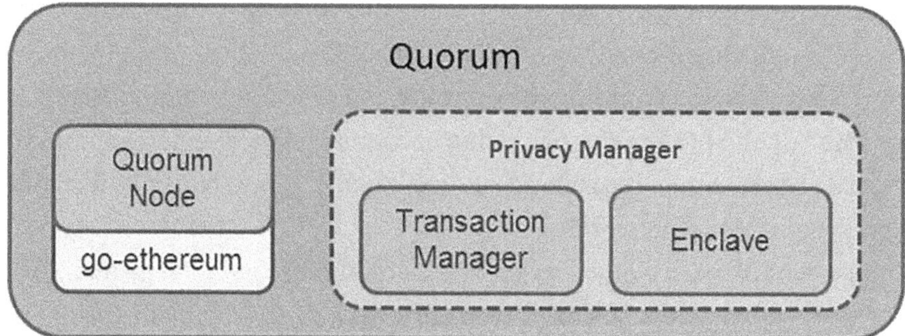

***Figure 5-4.** Quorum architecture*[4]

Quorum, a platform based on Ethereum, operates on a consortium model and allows users to perform confidential transactions and store private blockchain information. It provides a familiar working environment for Ethereum developers and delivers anonymity for enterprise installations on the cloud. Quorum provides a JSON-RPC API that is Ethereum-compatible and enables users to engage with the blockchain. Quorum offers interoperability with other Ethereum-compatible systems, allowing consortium members to communicate seamlessly. However, it faces similar scaling limitations as Ethereum and might require additional security measures to be put in place.

Designing the DLT Network

Several procedures are involved in creating a DLT network for cloud-based infrastructures; one must choose the appropriate DLT platform, set up the network architecture, and integrate it with cloud services.

[4] `https://github.com/Consensys/quorum`

Firstly, it is crucial to choose the suitable distributed ledger technology platform, as discussed in the previous section. Once the platform is selected, the subsequent task is to outline the network architecture. This involves choosing the appropriate level of confidentiality and protection for the network, determining the quantity and placement of nodes, and deciding on the method for achieving consensus. The network architecture should include integrating cloud services such as cloud computing, cloud storage, and cloud networking.

Integration with cloud services is essential for scalability, availability, and cost-effectiveness. Amazon Web Services (AWS), Microsoft Azure, and Google Cloud Platform (GCP) are cloud service providers that offer a range of services for deploying and managing DLT networks. Serverless computing, virtual machines, containers, and blockchain-as-a-service are examples of services that belong to this category.

Develop Smart Contracts

Developing smart contracts is essential for incorporating DLT into cloud-based infrastructures. Designing, writing, testing, and implementing self-executing contracts on a distributed ledger technology network are integral components of this procedure.

The initial stage of the development process involves outlining the requirements. During this phase, the development team closely engages with stakeholders to comprehend the objectives, requirements, and planned features. The team will now develop the architecture of the smart contract, incorporating data structures, functions, on-chain versus off-chain storage, and storage to ensure alignment with the project goals. Developers use programming languages like Solidity to write the logic of the smart contract. This logic determines the terms, conditions, and actions that are activated by specific triggers or inputs.

Once the developers finish writing the code, they simulate various scenarios to ensure the smart contract works as intended and is free from vulnerabilities, flaws, or logical errors that could compromise its functionality or security. This examination encompasses unit testing, integration testing, and security audits. Once the smart contract has been tested, it is published on the DLT network. This method involves assigning an address to the contract, allowing it to be accessed by interacting parties.

Smart contract creation relies on a diverse range of tools and technologies tailored for constructing, testing, deploying, and overseeing contracts inside distributed ledger technology environments. Smart contract development tools facilitate the process of writing, testing, and deploying smart contracts by offering essential functionalities. Ethereum, Binance Smart Chain (BSC), Cardano, Polkadot, Avalanche, and Solana are popular platforms for creating smart contracts.

Developers in the blockchain environment must follow best practices and coding standards to ensure the security, reliability, and performance of newly created smart contracts that utilize Web3 technology. This area encompasses the application of secure coding methodologies, adherence to known design patterns, and execution of extensive testing and security audits.

Testing and Validating

Ensuring that smart contracts are working correctly, testing network performance, and validating the functionality of APIs and network services are all components of this process. To automate the testing process, utilize a range of testing tools and frameworks.

Testing the integration of DLT network and cloud services should occur after both have been individually tested. Verifying the connectivity between the distributed ledger technology (DLT) network and cloud services, ensuring proper data flow, and certifying the accurate execution of smart contracts are key components of this procedure. Automating the testing process can be achieved by using different integration testing tools and frameworks.

Ensuring security is a crucial element of every integrated system. Therefore, it is necessary to conduct security assessments on the integrated DLT cloud infrastructure. This package encompasses testing for access limits, encryption, and network security.

It is crucial to also evaluate the efficiency of any integrated system. Thorough testing of the integrated DLT cloud infrastructure performance is essential. Testing for network latency, performance, and scalability is encompassed in this. Automating the testing process can be achieved by using a range of performance testing tools and frameworks.

Resilience in the face of a calamity is a crucial element of every interconnected system. Exhaustive testing of the disaster recovery capabilities of the integrated DLT cloud architecture is essential. This involves testing the failover, disaster recovery, and backup and restore procedures.

Compliance is a crucial element; it is crucial to extensively evaluate the compliance of the integrated DLT cloud architecture. This includes testing for regulatory compliance, industry standards, and best practices.

Deploy and Monitor

Monitoring involves tracking several metrics like resource utilization, transaction throughput, and network latency to identify potential issues or bottlenecks.

A diverse range of tools and methods can be utilized to monitor the DLT-integrated cloud architecture. You may monitor the performance and health of the cloud infrastructure using cloud-based monitoring services like Amazon CloudWatch or Google Stackdriver. You can access these services at no cost. These services can provide you with real-time analytics, logs, and alerts to quickly identify and resolve any issues that may occur.

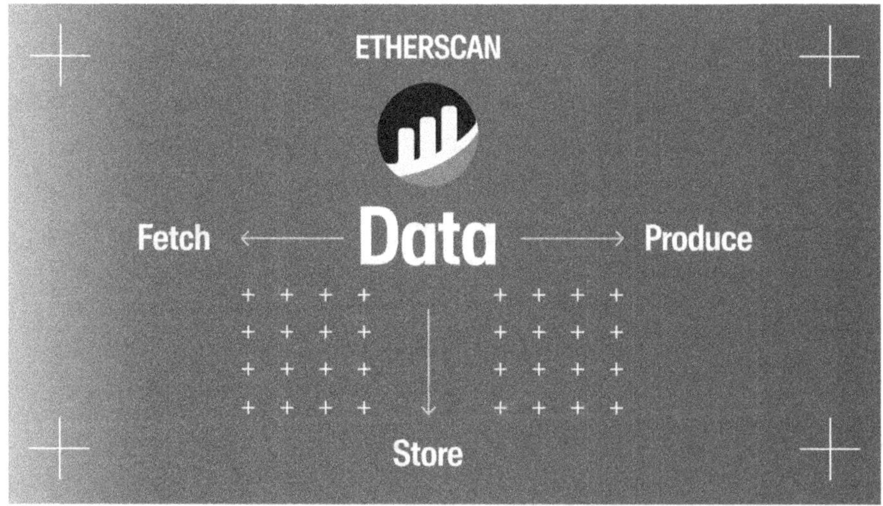

Figure 5-5. *Etherscan API workflow*[5]

You may monitor the performance and health of the DLT network using specialized monitoring tools like Etherscan for Ethereum or Fabric Analyzer for Hyperledger Fabric. These tools can offer insights into transaction volume, block propagation time, and smart contract execution, enabling you to enhance the performance of the distributed ledger technology network.

Various security monitoring tools can be used to ensure the safety of the DLT-integrated cloud architecture. These tools comprise intrusion detection systems (IDS) and security information and event management (SIEM) systems. They can help you detect and address security issues by monitoring network traffic, user behavior, and system records.

[5] https://www.moonpay.com/learn/cryptocurrency/what-is-etherscan#what-is-a-block-explorer

You can also choose to use automated monitoring and alerting systems to notify you of any issues or abnormalities that may arise in the system. You can utilize the monitoring and alerting services integrated into Kubernetes to oversee the health and performance of containerized applications.

Once testing is complete, deploy the integrated DLT cloud infrastructure in a production environment. Continuously monitor the system for any issues, and make adjustments as needed to optimize performance and security.

Architecture Considerations and Best Practices

To ensure a successful and safe deployment, it is crucial to consider many design aspects and best practices when combining distributed ledger technology with cloud-based infrastructure. The architecture must be designed to meet the specific needs of the DLT network and cloud services, while simultaneously prioritizing scalability, security, and high availability.

Choosing a cloud provider and infrastructure are crucial considerations. The cloud provider's infrastructure services must be strong and secure to meet the needs of the DLT network. The infrastructure should be designed to provide high availability and scalability, with redundant components and automatic failover methods. The infrastructure must support the performance needs of the distributed ledger technology network, such as low latency and high throughput.

Security is another crucial element to take into account. Encryption, access restrictions, and network partitioning are essential security measures that should be integrated into the design of the Ethereum DLT network and cloud infrastructure. The infrastructure should provide protection against distributed denial-of-service (DDoS) attacks as well as other security issues. The infrastructure should support regulatory compliance requirements, including data protection and privacy regulations.

Ensuring uninterrupted connection between the DLT network and cloud services is essential when integrating DLT with cloud services. Application Programming Interfaces (APIs) and other integration technologies may be used to accomplish this. To enable secure and reliable communication between the DLT network and cloud services, the APIs should be developed with features for data transformation, validation, and error management.

When creating smart contracts for DLT-integrated cloud infrastructure, it is essential to follow the best practices for smart contract development. These solutions include using secure coding practices, conducting thorough testing and validation, and following established design patterns. The smart contracts should be designed to provide clear and concise business logic, as well as support versioning and updates.

Comprehensive testing and validation of the infrastructure and smart contracts are essential to verify the integrated DLT cloud infrastructure. One can achieve this by using automated testing tools and frameworks, together with manual testing and validation systems. Functional testing, performance testing, and security testing should all be part of the testing duties.

Lastly, it is crucial to provide ongoing monitoring and maintenance of the infrastructure and smart contracts while setting up and overseeing the cloud infrastructure integrated with distributed ledger technology. This can be achieved by using monitoring tools, services, automatic notifications, and alerting systems. Monitoring should encompass compliance, security, and performance.

When integrating distributed ledger technology (DLT) with cloud-based infrastructure, it is crucial to carefully address architecture concerns and adhere to best practices. The infrastructure should be designed to facilitate seamless connectivity between the DLT network and cloud services, ensuring high availability, scalability, and security. When creating smart contracts, it is crucial to follow the best practices for secure coding and testing rigorously. Comprehensive testing, validation, continual monitoring, and maintenance are essential, and enterprises can achieve a successful and secure deployment of DLT-integrated cloud infrastructure by following these best practices.

CHAPTER 6

Challenges and Security

Considerations in Decentralized Implementations

We've looked at how distributed ledger technology (DLT) is designed, how it works in the real world, and how it could change many different businesses. On the other hand, putting decentralized systems into place comes with its own set of problems and safety issues, just like any other new technology. Understanding these problems, analyzing the security risks they pose, and suggesting ways to lower those risks are the main goals of this chapter. Furthermore, we will compare centralized systems with decentralized structures to make the pros and cons of each method stand out.

G. Deshmukh and S. M. Thameem Nizamudeen, *Decentralized Business*,
https://doi.org/10.1007/979-8-8688-0953-8_6

Technical Challenges of Decentralized Systems

Scalability

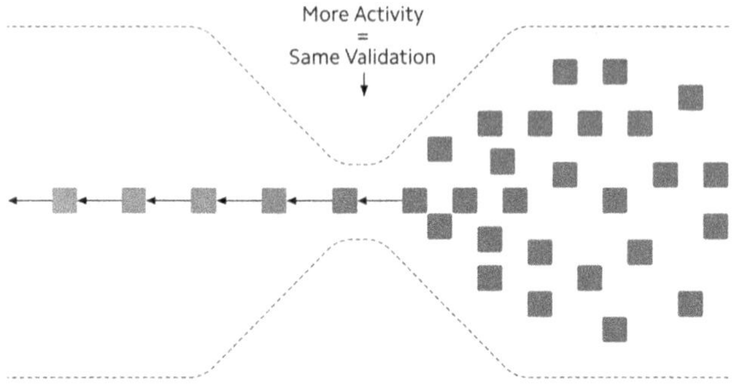

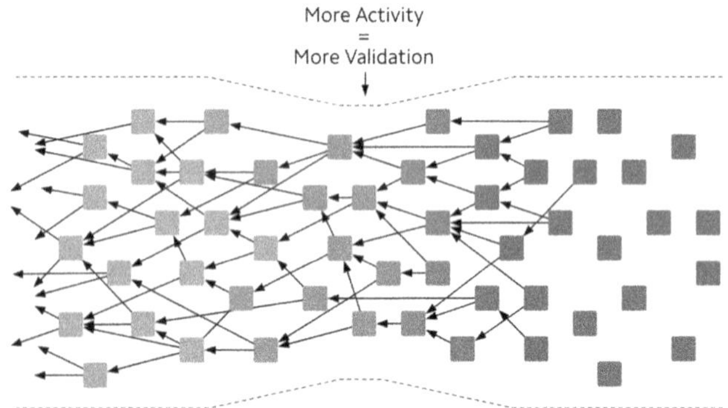

Figure 6-1. *Example of IOTA Tangle resolving scalability*[1]

[1] https://en.wikipedia.org/wiki/IOTA_%28technology%29#/media/File:Blockchain_vs_tangle_bottleneck.png

Scalability is a big problem for distributed ledger technology (DLT) because it makes it hard for the system to handle more users, transactions, and nodes without affecting its security, performance, or decentralization. Scalability is a major concern because it makes it hard for the system to work. One of the biggest problems that needs to be fixed is the slow transaction throughput, which causes traffic jams and longer transaction times. In addition, the problem is made even worse by the fact that the size of the blocks limits the number of transactions that can be stored in each block.

Network latency is another problem because it takes time for nodes to talk to each other and reach a consensus. The general performance of the network will be affected by how slowly this process goes. It might also take a huge amount of energy to run the network and do all the difficult calculations, so it becomes unsustainable. Furthermore, there is a big problem with the trade-off between scalability and security. In this case, boosting scalability often means lowering security and the other way around, too.

To solve these problems, a number of different approaches have been proposed. Some of these choices are sharding, off-chain transactions, second-layer scaling solutions, pruning, data compression, and making consensus methods work better. Sharding is the process of dividing a network into several parallel, smaller chains in order to increase transaction throughput and reduce latency. Off-chain transactions, on the other hand, must be finished off the main chain and settled on the main chain in batches to increase throughput. The adoption of second-layer scaling solutions, such as state channels or sidechains, can also result in increased transaction throughput and decreased latency.

By pruning and data compression, you can make storage more efficient and cut down on the size of the book. It is also possible to improve performance and lower the amount of energy used by the consensus algorithm.

Interoperability

Interoperability is a very important issue for distributed ledger technology (DLT). Interoperability means that different DLT systems can communicate with each other, share data, and do business with each other without any problems. The lack of connectivity is stopping a lot of people from using DLT. This is because it creates silos and limits the technology's benefits.

Making sure that DLT systems can communicate with each other is not easy. This is because different distributed ledger technology systems use different consensus methods. This means that they can't communicate with each other and agree on a single fact. Second, it's hard to move data from one DLT system to another because they use different data types. Third, the fact that DLT systems are not standardized makes it hard to make common interfaces and standards to fix problems with interoperability. Fourth, distributed ledger technology systems have different limits on how much they can grow. This makes it hard to handle transactions between systems with different capacities.

Interoperability makes it easier to attack because a weakness in one system can be used to get into other systems that have the same weakness.

There was research conducted that found some problems that come up with interoperability in the setting of digital ledger technologies (DLT) and Virtual Enterprises (VE). One of the biggest problems in VEs is that the sensors, tools, and devices are not all the same. To fully use the potential of DLTs, we need to make sure that all of these systems can work together and share data. This is called interoperability .

The fact that the world of distributed ledger technology is fragmented, which has led to the creation of new, different distributed platforms over the years, makes this problem even harder to solve. Different types of government, like permissioned and permissionless, have grown out of this fragmentation. These models make it harder for DLT to work with other systems, and they could lead to walls of digital assets and data that can't be shared between vendors.

Another problem is that different distributed ledgers are kept separate, which has created "silos" for assets and data. This makes it harder to use distributed ledger technology (DLT). Because of this, it is hard for different platforms that use distributed ledger technology to work and communicate with each other. This makes it harder for platforms that use distributed ledger technology to be used by more people. Cross-DLT communication is very complicated, and making cross-DLT tools work is also very hard.

Also, the solutions that have been suggested in the past for making DLT work with other systems, like naïve relay, sidechain, oracle solutions notary scheme, or relay chain, aren't usually used because they need a lot of resources or would be too expensive to run.

A smaller number of studies also look into the possible benefits and uses of external digital platforms and DLTs in Virtual Environments (VE). Also, it is not possible for DLTs to work with digital devices.

To solve the problems, it is suggested to use a layered framework to plan and create the stakeholders, technologies, and methods that work with both distributed ledger technology (DLT) and older systems. This makes it easy to share, connect, and transfer data.

The directed acyclic graph (DAG) protocol, which is what IOTA Tangle is based on, can help players in VE work together, both those who can be trusted and those who can't. IOTA Tangle was picked as a supporting DLT because it can track data that can't be changed and can't be tampered with. Because of these traits, it is possible to make an ecosystem that works with other systems.

Consensus Mechanism

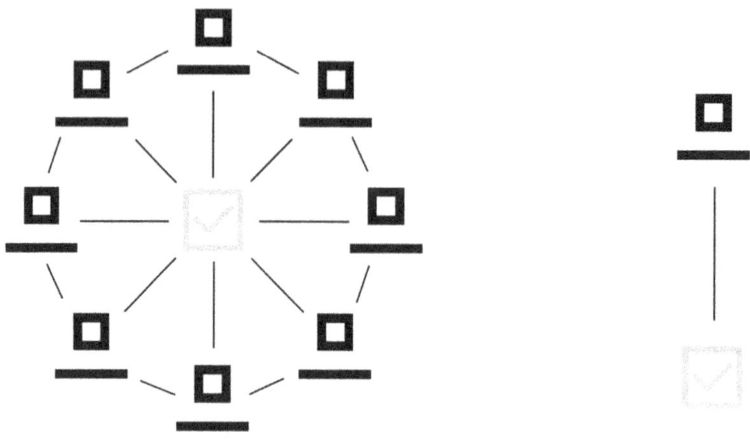

Figure 6-2. *Centralized vs. decentralized consensus*[2]

Although blockchains are distributed peer-to-peer systems that are open to anybody, no single entity can own or control them. Blockchains are accessible to everyone. Instead of relying on a reliable third party, agreement is achieved through the utilization of a consensus mechanism that permits the coordination of a peer-to-peer network that is distributed across multiple computer networks. As a result of the fact that both processes entail coordinating the actions of various parties and coming to an agreement on tasks and choices, the concept of corporate governance may take the form of consensus among various distributed parties in a centralized system.

[2] https://hacken.io/discover/consensus-mechanisms

It is of the utmost importance for a blockchain payments network to ensure that transactions are processed, settled, and validated accurately, as well as to reduce instances of double-spending. When it comes to blockchains, attaining consensus is an essential component of the way transactions are handled and decided upon. To put it another way, there are resources that are at stake, and attaining consensus in a blockchain network involves being able to arrive at a shared state while maintaining the distributed character of the network.

The foundation upon which they are built is the premise that all open public blockchains should be able to reach consensus throughout a distributed network, even when there are conflicts, without putting control in one location. Proof-of-work (PoW) and proof-of-stake (PoS) are the two algorithms that are most widely recognized for their ability to reach consensus.

The capacity of a distributed system to function successfully even when some of its components fail or behave maliciously is referred to as Byzantine fault tolerance (BFT). This is one of the most significant issues that must be overcome. BFT is essential in DLT and blockchain because rogue or unreliable nodes have the potential to interrupt or completely fail the system.

Distributed ledger technology (DLT) utilizes consensus as a means to construct fault-tolerant systems. This is accomplished by involving several nodes, known as voting nodes, which are required to reach a consensus on proposed transactions or particular outcomes. After they have reached a consensus, the conclusion that they have reached is believed to be final and cannot be changed.

DLT also presents a difficulty in the form of the CAP theorem. Consistency, availability, and partition tolerance are the three assurances that a distributed data store cannot concurrently give more than two of. According to the CAP theorem, it is impossible for a data store to deliver more than two of these guarantees at the same time. To ensure that the distributed ledger technology system functions in an appropriate manner, the consensus mechanism is accountable for enforcing the features of the CAP.

Several consensus mechanisms that are mainly targeting private/permissioned implementations include practical Byzantine fault tolerance (PBFT), democratic Byzantine fault tolerance (DBFT), Istanbul-BFT, redundant Byzantine fault tolerance (RBFT), delegated Byzantine fault tolerance (dBFT), Raft, and QuorumChain consensus. The exact requirements of the DLT system will determine which of these consensus processes is the most appropriate to use. Each of these mechanisms has both advantages and downsides.

Proof-of-work (PoW), proof-of-elapsed time (PoET), proof-of-weight (PoWeight), proof-of-stake (PoS), delegated proof-of-stake (DPoS), randomized proof-of-stake (RPoS), and leased proof-of-stake (LPoS) are some of the mechanisms primarily utilized in permissionless and public DLTs. These consensus algorithms come with their own set of difficulties, like the "nothing at stake" dilemma in proof-of-stake (PoS), which states that in the event of a fork, the best course of action for any miner is to participate in every chain. This ensures that the miner receives their reward regardless of which fork becomes the winner.

Privacy and Confidentiality

Businesses and the government are gathering huge amounts of data that have never been seen before in our fast-paced, data-driven world. It is thought that more than 50% of these data are secret. The Health Insurance Portability and Accountability Act (HIPAA), the Payment Card Industry Data Security Standard (PCI DSS), the General Licensing and Business Practices Act (GLBA), and European Privacy Laws are just a few examples of industry and governmental data privacy standards that safeguard this sensitive, private, financial, and health data. Should you fail to keep sensitive data safe, it could have a big effect on your business.

The Ponemon Institute did a study that found that the average cost of a data breach in 2012 was $194 per record. This means that each company lost $5.5 million. Despite this, data breaches have costs other than just money. When your customers lose trust in your business because of a data breach, it can be disastrous for your reputation and your business. A study also found that 69% of organizations find it hard to limit user access to sensitive information in business and IT settings.

Hence, in terms of privacy and confidentiality, DLT presents a number of obstacles. Distributed ledger technology is made to be both transparent and unchangeable on purpose. This means that data can't be changed or deleted after it has been saved. This could be a challenge when it comes to protecting sensitive data, like personal data, which must be updated or deleted on a regular basis to maintain privacy.

A network of nodes spread out across the world is used by DLT to verify and record transactions. This means that data is distributed across several nodes, increasing the risk of unauthorized access or data breaches.

DLT offers some privacy through the use of pseudonyms, but it is not entirely anonymous. Advanced techniques allow for the creation of a link between transactions and specific people, which could lead to those individuals' privacy being violated. Smart contracts are often used in distributed ledger technology. If these contracts are not made and put into place with privacy and confidentiality in mind before they are put into effect, they run the risk of revealing sensitive information.

Distributed ledger technology also has to follow many data privacy rules, such as the General Data Protection Regulation (GDPR) in the European Union. It can be hard to ensure compliance because distributed ledger technology is both decentralized and transparent.

To deal with these problems, it is important to put in place strong data security measures. Approaches that protect privacy, like zero-knowledge proofs and encryption, are examples of these kinds of methods. Additionally, it is crucial to maintain transparency and accountability in the operations of organizations that handle data, as well as to ensure compliance with the relevant data privacy rules.

Security Risks and Mitigation Strategies

51% Attacks

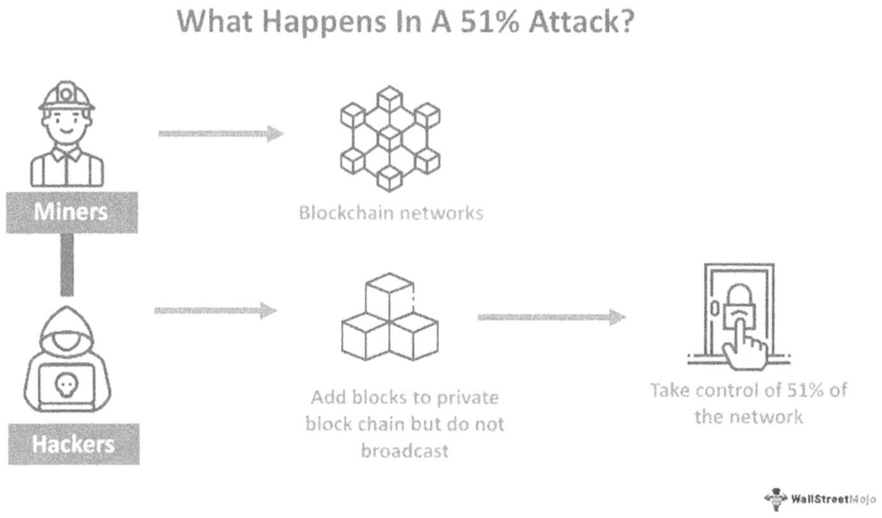

Figure 6-3. *51% attacks flow*[3]

A "51% attack" is an attack on a cryptocurrency blockchain that is done by a group of miners who control more than 50% of the network's total mining hash rate. If you own 51% of the nodes on the network, the people who control the network could possibly change the blockchain.

Attackers could ignore new transactions and stop them from getting confirmed. This would let them stop transfers between some users or all users. They would also be able to undo transactions that were made while they were in charge. These people could spend coins twice if they knew how to undo transactions. This is one of the problems that consensus systems like proof-of-work were made to solve. A 51% attack is more

[3] https://blockchainmagazine.net/unraveling-the-top10-blockchain-attacks-and-dlt-vulnerabilities

likely to happen when there are fewer miners on a Bitcoin network. This is because an attacker can easily get most of the hash rate since there are fewer people using it. The high cost of carrying out such an attack is a big reason why big cryptocurrencies like Bitcoin and Ethereum don't do it. However, attacks can still happen on smaller networks.

When it comes to distributed ledger technology, an attack that succeeds with a 51% share can cost companies a lot of money, hurt their image, and even get them in trouble with the law. When it comes to money, attackers can double-spend coins, which is the same thing as stealing money from people and businesses. Because of this, businesses that accept cryptocurrencies as payment or use them for private transactions may lose a lot of money.

Attacks with 51% of the votes can hurt the image of the distributed ledger technology network that is being attacked, which can make the network less valuable and less popular. People might not trust an organization if their activities depend on the network. This could hurt their image, which could hurt their business connections and customers' trust. In many places, businesses are required by law to follow certain rules when they deal with cryptocurrencies for business purposes. There could be legal consequences for a company that doesn't follow these rules or can't protect its clients' assets from a 51% attack.

A 51% attack on DLT networks is less likely to happen if companies take a number of precautions. Before they do anything else, they should spread their mining across several mining pools. That way, they won't have to rely on just one pool to confirm transactions. Because of this process, it is less likely that a single entity will be able to control the network's hash rate.

The second thing that companies should do to find possible security holes and fix them before they happen is to keep an eye on the health of the DLT network. This includes checking the number of active nodes and how the network's hash rate is spread out.

To avoid possible legal issues, organizations should stay up to date on the regulatory requirements that are associated with cryptocurrencies and ensure compliance with those laws. To lower the risk of a 51% attack, choose distributed ledger technology networks that have been around for a long time and have a large group of different types of miners.

Organizations can help make the DLT network safer by taking part in community discussions, spreading best practices, and supporting efforts to make the network more resilient. Furthermore, organizations will be better able to protect themselves from the threats that 51% of attacks on distributed ledger technology networks could bring.

Smart Contract Vulnerabilities

When it comes to distributed ledger technology (DLT), weak spots in smart contracts can pose major security risks to businesses. Speed, accuracy, reliability, and transparency are just a few of the many benefits they offer. Despite this, they also pose unique security risks because they can be used by bad actors, which can cost businesses money, hurt their image, and even lead to legal problems.

Smart contracts are vulnerable to reentrancy attacks and denial-of-service (DoS) attacks, in which an attacker floods the contract with too many transactions, making it unresponsive or unable to execute correctly. These holes can lead to transactions that aren't supposed to happen, data manipulation, and theft of digital assets, all of which can cost businesses a lot of money.

In order to lower the risks associated with vulnerabilities in smart contracts, organizations can adopt a number of best practices. Before they do anything else, they should make sure that they always use safe software development methods during the whole deal. This will make sure that the code is tried, reviewed, and audited carefully to find any possible security holes. To do this, you have to follow set rules for writing code, like the ones for smart contracts set by the Secure Software Development Framework (SSDF) and the Open Web Application Security Project (OWASP).

Second, businesses should create tracking tools to keep an eye on how contracts are being used and get alerts when users do something that isn't normal. And because of this, businesses can find and deal with possible threats as quickly as possible, which lowers the damage of any abuse that might happen. There are many kinds of tracking tools, such as intrusion detection systems, log analysis tools, and blockchain analytics platforms. These tools keep an eye on the trends of transactions and look for actions that might be fishy.

Businesses should think about the option of using formal proof tools to show the public that smart contracts are correct and safe. Number theory and computer programs that prove theorems are used to look over the code of the contract during formal proof. This method makes sure that the code works the way it was meant to without adding any security holes.

They should also make sure that their smart contracts are in line with both the laws that are already in place and the best practices in the field. This means following data protection laws like the General Data Protection Regulation (GDPR) and the California Consumer Privacy Act (CCPA), as well as setting up complete access controls and identity management systems to keep sensitive information safe.

Last but not least, companies should put in place strict security rules and controls to make sure their blockchain technology is safe. Putting in place strong Identity and Access Management (IAM) systems, doing regular risk assessments and audits, and making detailed emergency recovery plans that cover all the blockchain's possible threats are all parts of this. Companies that follow these best practices can lower the risks that come with weak spots in smart contracts and make sure that their DLT networks work safely and efficiently.

Sybil Attacks

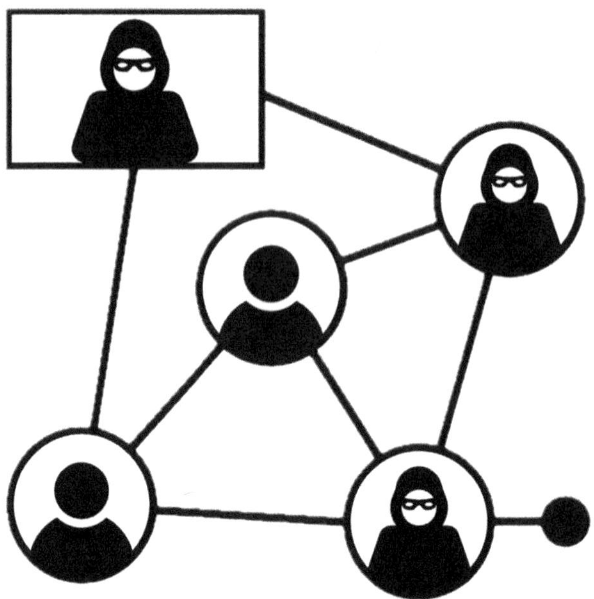

Figure 6-4. *Sybil attack network*[4]

A Sybil attack is one of the biggest security risks that companies face when they use distributed ledger technology (DLT). In a peer-to-peer network, a bad actor creates many fake identities or nodes in order to change the network's consensus process, stop it from working, or get access to sensitive data without permission

Sybil attacks can happen in many ways, such as by changing the network's transaction history, making the network unavailable, or using denial-of-service (DoS) attacks to stop genuine nodes from joining the network. As a result, these attacks can lead to transactions that aren't supposed to happen, data changes, and the theft of digital assets, all of which can cost businesses a lot of money.

[4] https://www.slideteam.net/sybil-attack-network-monotone-icon-in-powerpoint-pptx-png-and-editable-eps-format.html

There are a number of best practices that businesses can use to lower the risks that come with Sybil attacks. First, they need to set up strong identity and access control systems to make sure that only authorized nodes can connect to the network. Strong authentication and authorization systems, like public-key cryptography and digital signatures, are being used as one of these steps to make sure that every node is who it says it is and stop people from getting in without permission.

Organizations should build a network of nodes that is both diverse and spread out so that one body doesn't have as much power over the whole thing. Being sure that no one group can control the network's consensus method is one way to reach this goal. It is possible to do this by inviting a lot of different kinds of nodes to join the network.

Establish processes to find Sybil's attacks so that businesses can find them and stop future attacks. Two parts of this are keeping an eye on how the network works and looking for any odd patterns, like a sudden rise in the number of nodes or a lot of data coming from one node over the others. Machine learning algorithms, statistical analysis methods, and game-theoretic models can all be used to find Sybil attacks. Through the use of game theory, these systems find and mark possible Sybil attacks.

Businesses should set up strong network security measures; putting in place firewalls, intrusion detection systems, and other safety steps to keep people from getting into the network without permission is part of this. Also, to stop people from listening in on and messing with network data, businesses should set up safe ways for nodes to talk to each other. Message protocols that are encrypted are one example of this kind of communication route.

Organizations should also come up with clear rules and basic principles for how nodes can join the network. This process includes describing the requirements for node eligibility, establishing rules for node behavior, and defining the consequences for failing to reach these rules. Organizations can reduce the risk of Sybil attacks by establishing clear standards and guidelines that ensure all nodes interact with the network in a fair and transparent way.

Data Tampering

Data tampering is a big security risk for companies that use distributed ledger technology because it can change how accurate and trustworthy the data is that is stored on the ledger. It occurs when data is changed or edited without permission. Distributed ledger technologies are not entirely resistant to tampering, however, despite their architecture. Hackers could use flaws in the DLT system to change data, which could have very bad effects on businesses.

Data tampering can happen in a number of ways, such as by changing transaction data, the consensus process, or smart contracts. This could happen if someone had changed the transaction data to move digital assets without permission, which would cost everyone money. The hacker can also change the consensus method to take over the network for distributed ledger technology. The data that is saved on the ledger can now be changed by them. Attackers can also use flaws in smart contracts to change how they work, which can lead to actions that neither party meant.

In DLT, organizations can lower the risks of data tampering by following a number of best practices. They should first set up efficient access controls and identity management systems to make sure that only authorized parties can see and change the data saved on the ledger. This includes putting in place strong systems for identity and authorization, like digital signatures and public-key cryptography. These methods are used to make sure that everyone is who they say they are and to stop people from getting in without permission.

A network could be established of nodes that are both diverse and spread out so that one body doesn't have as much power over the whole thing. One way to reach this goal is to ensure that no one group can control the network's consensus method. It is possible to do this by inviting a lot of different kinds of nodes to join the network.

Companies should develop ways to ensure accurate data integrity to find and stop data tampering, such as implementing hash functions, digital signatures, and other types of cryptography. These methods are used to make sure that the data on the ledger is accurate and unaltered. Additionally, businesses should set up monitoring tools to keep an eye on any changes that are made to data and get alerts for any strange behavior.

By installing firewalls, intrusion detection systems, and other safety steps to keep people from getting into the network without permission, organizations could set up a safe communication channel between nodes to stop people from listening in on and tampering with network data. Message protocols that are encrypted are one example of this kind of communication route.

It is imperative for businesses to make clear rules and guidelines for how to handle data in the DLT network. Outlining the requirements for data to be included, setting rules for how data should behave, and explaining what will happen if these rules are broken are all parts of this process. The likelihood of data tampering or other types of network manipulation can be reduced by organizations having clear standards and guidelines to ensure that all participants join the network fairly and transparently.

In conclusion, decentralized implementations have a lot of potential to change many different industries by promoting trust, transparency, and inclusivity. Even so, it is essential to fix the technical issues and safety worries that come with distributed ledger technologies so that they can fully live up to their potential. People who have a stake in decentralized systems can handle their complexity and build strong, safe communities for the future if they use new ideas and follow the best practices.

CHAPTER 7

Web3 Strategies for Cloud Professionals

Web3 is becoming well-known among cloud professionals as it marks the start of a new era for the Internet based on DLT technology. This open form of the Internet is likely to cause big changes in how data is stored, managed, and accessed. Knowledgeable cloud professionals who are familiar with Web3 technologies will be better able to help their companies take advantage of the new opportunities this paradigm shift brings.

Decentralized applications (dApps) now offer better privacy, security, and dependability than regular web apps. Professionals in the cloud who are familiar with Web3 technologies will have an edge in helping their companies create and release decentralized applications (dApps) that take advantage of these benefits. Web3 also uses smart contracts to automate many business processes, eliminating the need for intermediaries and increasing efficiency. As more businesses look to use this technology, there will be an increasing need for cloud professionals who know how to make and use smart contracts.

G. Deshmukh and S. M. Thameem Nizamudeen, *Decentralized Business*,
https://doi.org/10.1007/979-8-8688-0953-8_7

Strategic Opportunities for Cloud Professionals

Web3 gives cloud professionals interesting and broad strategic choices. Web3, the next step in the evolution of the Internet, brings about new ownership, incentive, and community models that could completely change how cloud professionals work and connect with their clients.

Creation of dApps

Due to the increased security, privacy, and resilience that these dApps bring, cloud professionals who are familiar with Web3 technologies will be in high demand to help businesses create and implement them. The following table is from the dApp Development Frameworks page of the Ethereum documentation, which gives an overview of the various frameworks available to develop dApps on Ethereum.

Table 7-1. *Table of dApp Development Frameworks*[1]

Framework	Language(s) Supported	Key Features	Intended Use Case
Foundry	Solidity	Fast, modular toolkit, supports local blockchain instance, compilation, and testing	General Ethereum application development
Hardhat	Solidity, JavaScript	Professional-grade development environment, debugging, testing, deployment	Professional Ethereum dApp development
Web3j	Java	Jamaica Virtual Machine-based blockchain application development	Blockchain application development on JVM
ethers-kt	Kotlin, Java, Android	Async, high-performance library for EVM-based blockchains	Development of applications of EVM-based blockchain on Kotlin/Java/Android
Create Eth App	JavaScript	Simple setup for Ethereum-powered apps with UI frameworks and DeFi templates	Fast way of making Ethereum apps
Scaffold-Eth	JavaScript, TypeScript	Wrap of Ethers.js, Hardhat and React to build dApps	Kickstart your Ethereum dApp with already set up tools
The Graph	Many	Efficient querying of blockchain data	Data indexing and querying for decentralized applications
Alchemy	Multiple	Full-suite Ethereum development platform with state of the art tools	Ethereum dApp and infrastructure development
NodeReal	Multiple	High scalability and high-performance Ethereum development platform	High performance in developing on Ethereum
Chainstack	Multiple	Web3 development platform supporting multiple blockchains	Multi-blockchain dApp development
Crossmint	Multiple	Enterprise-grade platform for multi-chain NFT application development	Development of NFT applications on Major EVM chains
Brownie	Python	Python-based development environment and testing framework	Python developers building and testing smart contracts
Truffle	JavaScript, Solidity	Full suite of development, testing, and deployment environment	Full-featured Ethereum dApps development
Covalent	Multiple	Providing blockchain data via enriched APIs for 200+ chains	Get access to blockchain data and insights for multiple chains
Wake	Python	Framework agnostic all-in-one tool for contract testing, fuzzing, deployment, vulnerability scanning, code navigation	Full-suite smart-contract test and security analysis

[1] https://ethereum.org/en/developers/docs/frameworks

Smart Contracts

Another strategic possibility is the use of smart contracts, which could automate many business processes and replace the need for intermediaries. Cloud professionals who understand how to create and use smart contracts to increase productivity and profitability can help organizations significantly. The following table is from the dApp Development Frameworks page of the Ethereum documentation, which gives an overview of the various frameworks available to develop smart contracts on Ethereum.

***Table 7-2.** Table of smart contract development frameworks*[2]

Framework	Language(s) Supported	Key Features	Intended Use Case
Ape	Python	Smart contract development for users in Python, data scientists, and security professionals	Smart contract development with Python
Tenderly	Solidity, Vyper	Web3 development platform, testing, debugging, monitoring, improving dApp UX	Full lifecycle management of smart contracts and dApps
OpenZeppelin SDK	Solidity	Tooling to develop, compile, upgrade, and deploy smart contracts	Secure and upgradeable smart contract development
thirdweb SDK	Multiple	SDKs and CLI for interacting with smart contracts	Simplified interaction with smart contracts in web3 applications
Brownie	Python	Python-based development environment and testing framework	Python developers building and testing smart contracts
Catapulta	Multiple	Multi-chain smart contract deployment tool, automated verifications, deployment tracking	Automated and multi-chain smart contract deployment

[2] `https://ethereum.org/en/developers/docs/frameworks`

Development of Digital Assets

Web3 also enables the development of new types of digital assets, such as non-fungible tokens (NFTs) and decentralized finance (DeFi) applications. Businesses can expect these new asset classes to bring about new possibilities and possibly problems for established financial systems. Knowledgeable cloud professionals who are also familiar with Web3 technologies will be able to help their companies through this change and make the most of the opportunities these new assets offer.

New Ownership and Transactional Models

Web3's new ownership and transactional models could give users more power and make their relationships with brands stronger. Professionals in the cloud who are familiar with how to use these models will be able to help their companies come up with new products and services that meet the changing needs and wants of customers.

Decentralized Storage

Web3 technologies open the door for decentralized storage options, which may offer better privacy, security, and cost savings than traditional cloud storage. Companies can design and implement these systems with the help of cloud professionals who are familiar with decentralized storage solutions in order to reduce their reliance on centralized cloud providers. The InterPlanetary File System (IPFS) is the foundational technology to grasp when considering decentralized storage—a key piece of the overall Web3 ecosystem.

Content-Addressed Data

Traditional file storage systems and cloud storage solutions locate files based on where they're kept—on a specific path or an address, such as a URL or a file path.

IPFS approach storage by doing content addressing. A unique identifier, based on the content of each file, is called CID, the abbreviation for content identifier. That is how the pulling of files happens by their content and not by their location. Whenever the content changes, its CID must be changed to ensure the guarantee of data being immutable and hence verifiable.

Peer-to-Peer Network

In centralized storage systems, data rests on servers owned and controlled by one entity, say Google or Amazon. IPFS is a P2P network wherein every file is fragmented into bits residing across millions of nodes in the overall network, as defined in earlier chapters "decentralized" way. In other words, every node can store files and share them, thereby making it resilient to the entire network and resistant to censorship.

Decentralization and Redundancy

Under IPFS, the same file is copied onto a number of nodes. As long as at least one of these nodes possesses that file, data is always available against some shutting down. There is no central server to count on; therefore, IPFS removes the single point of failure that reduces the risk of any single entity controlling or censoring data.

Efficiency Through Deduplication

Since IPFS uses content addressing, if many users upload the same file, the network will keep only one copy. Hence, the space required in the network is reduced.

Versioning and Mutability

Immutable data is data that doesn't change. IPFS allows for versioning, thus enabling one to track changes over time to multiple file versions. Mutable links give IPFS its mutability through the Interplanetary Name System, IPNS, which, at different instances in time, points to different CIDs. This way, users can update their content without having to update any link they may wish to share.

Use Cases for Decentralized Storage

Web3 applications are the projects related to Web3, be it dApps or blockchain platforms like Filecoin, which utilize the decentralized data storage and sharing properties of IPFS.

Normally, non-fungible tokens (NFTs) that reflect some digital content, such as images and videos, resort to IPFS for hosting in a decentralized, tamper-proof manner.

IPFS allows the archival and backup of important data, making them available in instances where original sources are taken down or altered.

Privacy and Security

Users are allowed to encrypt files before uploading them onto IPFS, so that only those with a decryption key will be able to retrieve the content.

While IPFS enforces no privacy—all data is public unless encrypted—it allows such a privacy-preserving storage to be created when combined with encryption and access control mechanisms.

Overall, IPFS is a powerhouse for decentralized storage that unlocks resilient, efficient, and censorship-resistant methods of data storage and publication. By transitioning from location-based to content-based addressing, it leverages a peer-to-peer network's strengths and opens a new paradigm for data storage better aligned with the decentralization and user empowerment principles at the heart of Web3.

Decentralized Identity Management

Cloud professionals who are familiar with decentralized identity management can help organizations build and set up decentralized systems, improving the user experience and reducing the risk of data breaches.

Decentralized Computing

Web3 technologies open the door to decentralized computing solutions, which might be more dependable and scalable than the old cloud technology. With the help of cloud professionals who are familiar with decentralized computing, businesses can design and implement these systems, increasing their ability to handle enormous tasks and reducing their reliance on centralized cloud providers.

Decentralized Finance

Decentralized finance (DeFi) systems enabled by Web3 technologies have the ability to be more open and transparent compared to more conventional banking systems. Hiring cloud professionals who are familiar with DeFi to build and set up these systems can help businesses offer financial services to more people.

Decentralized Governance

Decentralized governance solutions made possible by Web3 technologies may be more open and accountable than more traditional types of government. With the help of cloud professionals who are familiar with decentralized governance, organizations can design and implement these systems, improving their ability to make decisions in an open and honest way.

How to Excel in Decentralized Systems

Being an expert in decentralized systems like Web3 requires a thorough understanding of the theoretical underpinnings, practical experience, and technological knowledge. Initially, it is essential to understand how DLT technology works because it is the basis of decentralized systems. You have to learn about DLT's past to get a sense of its background, what it can do, and its pros and cons.

When it comes to DLT technology, decentralization means moving power and decision-making from one organization to a network of nodes that are spread out. Decentralized systems have a number of benefits over centralized ones, including increased security, transparency, and resistance to control. However, they might need specific knowledge and skills, and they might be harder to build and run.

DLT can run decentralized applications thanks to a group of technologies called Web3. It comes with smart contracts, decentralized computers, and storage. You need to learn about these technologies to know how they work together.

Getting things done is the best way to learn. Try to find ways to contribute to decentralized efforts, whether it's through your current position, open-source initiatives, or the creation of your own. There are many online tools that can help you get started with Web3 development. Some of these are tutorials, documentation, and online groups. Another great way to learn more about the field and improve your own skills is to join online groups and meet with other Web3 developers. Join online groups, go to conferences and meetups, and get involved in your community to stay on top of the latest news and trends.

You can make connections with other Web3 professionals by being a part of the group and learning from each other's life experiences and skills. This can help you stay in touch with other experts in the field and continue learning about decentralized systems.

Be sure to keep up with the latest findings. In the field of decentralized systems, which is characterized by quick evolution, new studies and developments are constantly being conducted. Read scholarly studies, go to conferences, and follow important people in your field to stay one step ahead of the curve. By keeping up with the latest research and developments, you can position yourself as an expert on decentralized systems and a leader in the field.

In this domain, you also have to learn about systems of incentives and governance. The use of these methods is essential in decentralized systems for bringing someone's interests to a consensus. You need to learn how to create systems that are both fair and effective by applying Decentralized Autonomous Organizations (DAOs) and other types of governance.

Decentralized systems use governance models to make decisions and keep tabs on the network. The interests of the participants are similar, and they are encouraged to contribute to the network through reward schemes. You must understand these concepts if you want to design and manage a decentralized system.

Some of the main ideas that these systems are based on are self-sovereignty and transparency. Take the time to really understand these ideas and think about how you can use them to make systems that are fair for everyone.

In decentralized systems, there is both a philosophical and a technological answer. By becoming familiar with their core beliefs and principles, you can learn more about the possibility for decentralized systems to change the world.

By following these guidelines, you can learn the skills and information required to succeed in the decentralized Web3 ecosystem. This is an interesting topic that is changing quickly. Remember that learning is something that you do for the rest of your life.

Career Prospects in Web3 (for Cloud Professionals)

Cloud professionals can look for a variety of jobs in the Web3 ecosystem, a decentralized digital economy built on DLT. The following are some of the career opportunities that cloud professionals in Web3 could have:

DLT Cloud Engineer

DLT cloud engineers plan, build, and run the infrastructure for DLT on cloud systems. It is important for them to know about cloud computing, DLT technology, and distributed systems. They need to make sure that the infrastructure for DLT is safe, can handle more users, and is always available.

Smart Contract Developer

Smart contract developers make and share smart contracts that can be used on DLT systems. They are expected to know a lot about programming languages like Solidity and DLT systems like Ethereum. Their job is to make sure the smart contracts are safe, work well, and meet the company's goals.

DLT Cloud Architect

A DLT cloud architect's job is to plan and oversee the use of DLT-based cloud systems. To do well, they need to know a lot about DLT technology, cloud computing, and business processes. Their job is to ensure that the DLT technology helps the business reach its goals.

DLT Security Specialist

DLT security specialists are in charge of keeping DLT technology safe and secure. They should be very familiar with compliance rules and knowledgeable about security measures and best practices. They implement security measures like encryption, filters, and access limits.

DLT Consultant

Companies that want to use DLT technologies can get help and advice from DLT consultants. They work closely with clients to understand their business needs and provide advice on the best DLT strategies. DLT consultants need to be able to think critically and solve problems while also being familiar with the newest DLT technologies.

Beyond these roles, cloud professionals can look for DeFi opportunities in other Decentralized Autonomous Organizations (DAOs), non-fungible tokens (NFTs), and decentralized finance. As quickly as these areas are growing, they offer cloud professionals exciting new ways to use their skills creatively.

To be successful in their jobs, cloud professionals need to be knowledgeable about DLT technology and its applications. They should also be able to work well under pressure and in a workplace that is always changing. Clear communication and quick problem-solving skills are also essential.

Cloud professionals can learn the skills and information they need through various training programs, certifications, and online resources. They can try to get certifications like certified DLT solution architect, certified Ethereum developer, and certified DLT security professional. People in the Web3 environment can also join online forums, groups, and conferences to stay up to date on the latest news and trends.

CHAPTER 8

Case Studies

Successful Transitions

As decentralization and the use of distributed ledger technology spread through more businesses and sectors, the world is going through a huge change. This change is being made because of a desire for more openness, safety, and efficiency in operations, as well as to give people and groups more autonomy.

Many areas, including banking, healthcare, energy, supply chain management, and identity verification, are moving toward decentralization. Decentralized systems in finance are changing the way peer-to-peer trades work by getting rid of the need for middlemen and making transactions much faster and safer. DLTs are being used in supply chain management to keep an eye on how materials and goods are moving. This makes things more clear and lowers the risk of fraud. More and more attention is being paid to creating decentralized health records and medical study platforms in the medical field. These improvements are meant to make it easier to handle patient data and help researchers work together.

The energy business is also moving toward decentralization. Blockchain-based energy trading sites are making it possible for people to buy and sell extra energy directly with each other. With the rise of autonomous identity management systems, identity verification is taking big steps forward. These systems give people power by letting them

G. Deshmukh and S. M. Thameem Nizamudeen, *Decentralized Business*,
https://doi.org/10.1007/979-8-8688-0953-8_8

manage their own personal information and making sure that they are authenticated safely. There are also more and more decentralized social media platforms that are popping up as options to the more common centralized platforms. The goal of these new platforms is to give users more control over their data and how they connect with others online.

Authorities and organizations are firmly supporting autonomy and incorporating DLT into their work. Central banks are looking into how DLT could be used for payment systems and digital currencies. At the same time, land registries are using blockchain technology to make sure that records of who owns land are safe and clear. New voting platforms are being made to make sure that elections are fair and safe, and new educational platforms are giving students more control over their school records and certificates.

DLTs are being used more and more in business because they have many benefits, including keeping records that can't be manipulated and being open to everyone, making things safer and lowering the risk of fraud, increasing efficiency and automation, making it easier for people to work together and share data, and giving people and groups more power. People, companies, and governments will all have to change how they do things in big ways as the world moves toward decentralization and DLT integration.

Still, this change comes with its own set of challenges, such as the need to set up regulatory frameworks, deal with worries about scalability, and spread education and awareness. As the use of autonomy and DLTs grows, it is important for everyone involved to work together to solve these problems so that the move to a more decentralized world goes smoothly. Beyond a certain point, adding DLTs to the global economy has a huge potential to make it fairer, safer, and more efficient. People would have more control over their important data and assets.

Let's further dive into how the modern world is exploiting DLTs and decentralization to its advantage.

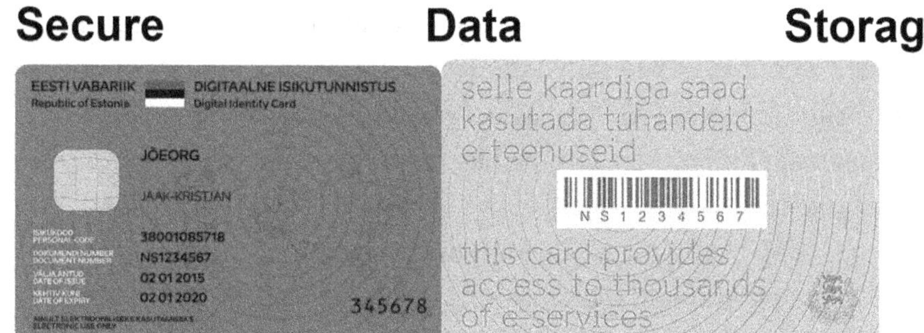

Figure 8-1. *Front and back image of Estonia's eID card*[1]

Estonia's eID System

Estonia has become one of the world's leaders in using distributed ledger technologies to keep track of digital identities. Blockchain technology is used to build the country's eID system, which lets people safely access many government services online and sign papers digitally.

The eID system is an important part of Estonia's digital society because it makes sure that people can use the Internet safely and easily. Customers can easily get to many government services online through this method. These services include healthcare, education, and taxes. With their eID, people can safely prove who they are and easily use these services from anywhere in the world.

The eID system is built on a blockchain infrastructure, which makes it a safe and decentralized way to handle digital identities. The system stores and manages identity information using a distributed ledger. This makes sure that everyone has fair access to the data and can verify digital identities.

[1] https://en.wikipedia.org/wiki/Estonian_identity_card

People can also digitally sign papers with their eID. This is a safe and legally binding way to sign contracts and other documents online. These results are important because they can help make a lot of different processes safer and more effective, like making contracts, doing business, and going to court.

Estonia's eID system goes beyond the basic framework and provides a very advanced and safe way to handle digital identities. Multi-factor identification, encryption, and a full legal framework for digital signatures are just a few of the advanced security features built into the system. These features make sure that the eID system is safe, reliable, and legal. This makes it a very useful tool for handling digital identities and helping to make the Internet a safer and more organized place.

Honduras' Public Land Record System

Honduras has worked with a blockchain technology company to look into how DLT could be used to create a secure and public land record system. The goal of this project is to solve problems like land disputes, bad property management, and landlords not being able to get credit.

In many developing countries, like Honduras, land registration systems aren't always accurate and can be hacked. This means that landowners are open to disputes and seizures that aren't legal. Honduras wants to use blockchain technology to make a system for recording land rights that can't be changed and is spread out across many computers. This will make sure that info about who owns a piece of property is safe and clear.

In order for the land register system to work, digital signatures for each land title transaction are recorded and timestamped on a distributed ledger. This method creates a clear and permanent record of who owns what, which reduces the chance of fraud and arguments. In addition, the system can include GPS measurements, which make it possible to precisely define the size of each piece of land. This function makes the registry much more accurate and reliable.

The idea to give landowners in Honduras titles holds a lot of promise for them and gives them a chance to make a lot of money. Landowners can use their digital land titles as collateral for loans if the land record system works well and is clear. This can make it much easier for people to get credit. This can help the economy grow and develop by giving landowners the freedom to spend in their homes and businesses.

When Honduras adopts blockchain technology, it joins a growing group of countries and organizations that see the huge potential of DLT to change many fields, including land registration, vote systems, medical record management, and trade finance. The use of DLT in these activities can lead to better safety, openness, and efficiency, which will eventually benefit people, businesses, and governments all over the world.

Supply Chain Management

Walmart's Food Tracking System

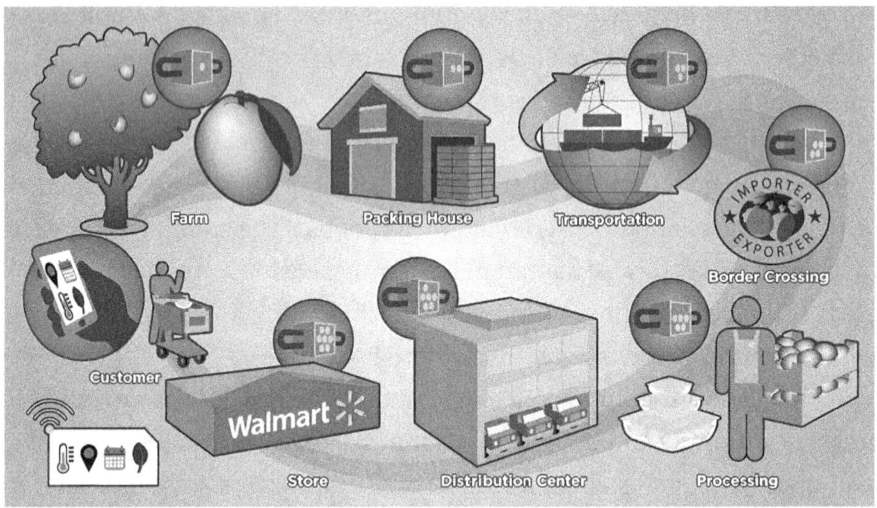

Figure 8-2. *Blockchain flow from farm to fork*[2]

Walmart is using distributed ledger technology to keep track of food from the farm to the table. This will help them find and fix problems with possible contamination more quickly. Blockchain technology and the Internet of Things (IoT) are used in this system to make the whole food supply chain fully traceable and clear.

Inputting this DLT-based system into action gives Walmart the ability to keep an eye on food goods in real time, tracking them from the farm where they are grown to the store where they are sold. This lets them quickly find the source of any contamination problems, cutting the time it takes to respond to food safety worries from weeks to seconds.

[2] https://www.altoros.com/blog/blockchain-at-walmart-tracking-food-from-farm-to-fork

The method works by recording different pieces of information, like the farm's location, the number of the lot, and the date of harvest. This creates an accurate and unchangeable record of the food's journey. This information is kept on a decentralized record, which makes sure that everyone in the supply chain has equal access to it and can see how the product is moving at all times.

This has a phenomenal influence on food safety that comes from Walmart using DLT-based tracking. The method could lower the risk of foodborne illnesses and improve people's health by making it faster to find and fix contamination problems. The method can also help build trust among customers and make the food supply chain work better by making things more clear and easy to track.

Financial Services

Ornua: Substituting LCs

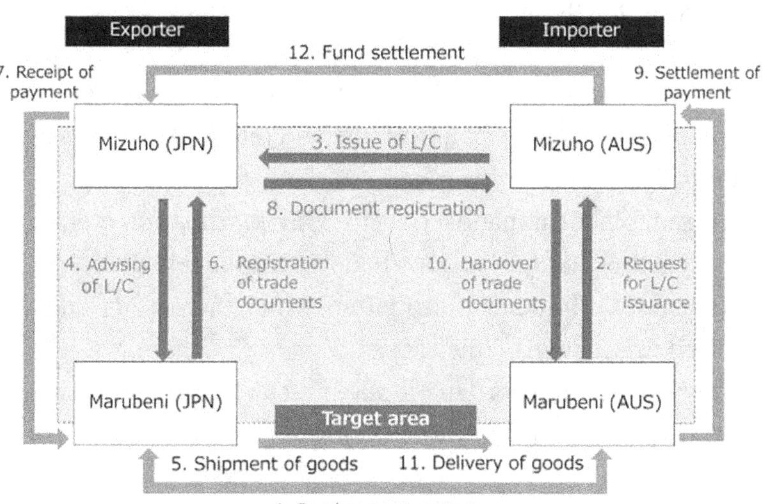

Figure 8-3. *Trade finance flow at Deutsche Bank*[3]

[3] https://flow.db.com/trade-finance/trade-finance-and-the-blockchain-three-essential-case-studies

An Irish dairy cooperative called Ornua ran into a big problem when it tried to sell to other countries. Letters of Credit (LCs) were traditionally used to ease trade finance, but this process was slow, complicated, and inefficient. When banks, exporters, and importers trade physical papers with each other, the process can take a long time, which can cause delays and make mistakes more likely.

To solve this issue, Ornua worked with Deutsche Bank to check out an LC option based on blockchain. The goal was to turn the whole process, from issuing the LC to receiving payment, into a safe and clear digital platform.

A decentralized ledger was used by the blockchain-based system to record and authenticate all transactions. This made sure that everyone had access to the same information at the same time. This got rid of the need for paper records and made it possible for banks, exporters, and importers to share data quickly and safely.

A lot of great things were done for the test project. The blockchain-based LC solution cut the processing time from 10 days to just a few hours, which made Ornua's export processes much faster and more efficient. The digital platform has made things much more clear and reduced the chance of mistakes, making it a very safe and reliable way to do business internationally.

The digital platform made it easy to share information quickly, which cut the time it took to process from 10 days to just a few hours. All sides had real-time access to the same information, which increased transparency and reduced the chance of mistakes.

The decentralized record made sure that all transactions were completely safe and honest, which greatly reduced the chances of fraud and cyber threats. The digital platform also got rid of the need for physical documents, which cut down on the costs of printing, shipping, and keeping them.

The pilot project's success has made it possible for more blockchain-based LC solutions to be used in the trade finance business. By working together with Deutsche Bank, Ornua has shown how blockchain technology can completely change the way trade finance is done, making it faster, safer, and more efficient.

Election Voting Systems

Utah County's Blockchain-Based Voting System

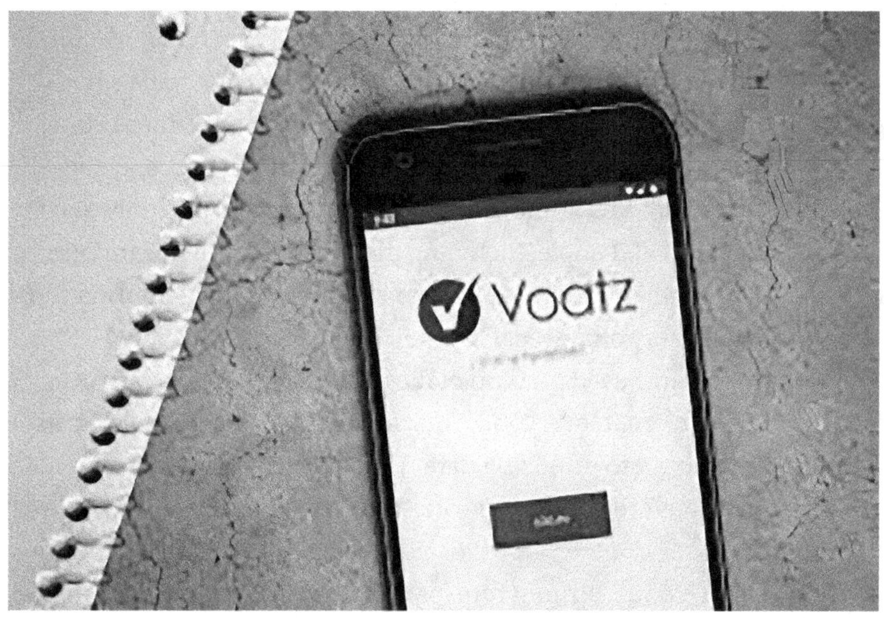

Figure 8-4. *Login screen of voting app—Voatz*[4]

[4] https://statescoop.com/utah-county-utah-begins-review-of-mobile-app-votes

By switching to a cutting-edge voting method based on blockchain, Utah County has made a huge step toward decentralization. Thanks to the Voatz app, the county's cutting-edge blockchain-based voting system lets eligible voters safely and easily cast their votes from anywhere in the world. This new technology is very helpful for foreign voters who used to have to use unsafe email voting methods that made it harder for them to keep their ballots private.

With the Voatz app, a voter's smartphone becomes a "ballot-marking device" that sends a digital record of their vote to a center that counts the votes. That's when the county's system makes a copy of the digital receipt in the old-fashioned paper ballot style. This method makes sure that every vote is correctly recorded and counted.

The blockchain technology that powers the Voatz app makes it possible to see for sure that votes cast from outside of the United States are real. The user is given a unique identification number after giving their vote. After that, this number can be checked against a public record to make sure it is real. People, including the voter, can use this unique identification number, which doesn't contain any personal information, to prove that the county office received their vote correctly.

The blockchain-based method makes the auditing process easy to understand and open to everyone. You can look at individual blocks in the blockchain to get to protected data. This data can then be decrypted to see if candidates are getting the votes they should from people all over the world.

With a higher voter turnout rate for people living outside of Utah County compared to people who live in the county, the blockchain-based voting method has shown promise. This revolutionary idea has the ability to completely change the voting process, making sure that everyone, no matter where they are, can take part in a safe, private, and reliable voting system.

Healthcare

Medchain

Medchain[5] is a blockchain tool that was made to store and share medical records of patients safely. It provides a decentralized and safe way to handle private healthcare data. The platform gives patients full control over their data and lets them choose which healthcare providers can access it. This makes it easier to handle medical records and protects patient data.

Medchain's pilot project in Dubai is a big step toward making it easier and safer for healthcare organizations to handle patient data. The project aims to solve the problems that come with traditional paper medical notes, which can be lost, damaged, or accessed by people who aren't supposed to.

Blockchain technology is used by the Medchain app to create a decentralized and very safe database of patient medical records. The use of DLT by the platform ensures the safe storage of patient data, allowing only authorized healthcare providers to view it. Patients will be able to keep control of their info and their privacy will be protected.

Medchain's platform makes it much easier to handle medical records, which means that accessing and sharing patient data takes a lot less time and effort. In order to make medical diagnoses and treatments more accurate and efficient, the platform lets healthcare workers quickly and easily access patient medical records.

The results of the pilot project in Dubai have been positive. For example, healthcare providers have seen better privacy for patient data and better handling of medical records. The platform's use of blockchain technology has also shown a lower risk of data breaches and unauthorized access. This makes the handling of sensitive healthcare data safer and more reliable.

[5] https://medicalchain.com/en/company-blog

Smart Contracts

Smart Contracts in Freight Invoice Management

Walmart Canada and DLT Labs[6] successfully set up a distributed ledger technology (DLT) system using Hyperledger Fabric to completely change the way they handle freight invoices. Smart contracts were used in this new strategy to make the complicated and often disputed process of freight bills easier.

Due to the complicated nature of price, extra charges, and variable costs, the freight transportation business isn't very efficient. For example, up to 70% of invoices are disputed. Walmart Canada works with many shipping companies to make sure that goods get to its 400+ stores across the country quickly. Even so, the process of billing for freight by hand and on paper led to mistakes, delays, and arguments, which cost a lot of money and wasted time.

DLT Labs has made a tool that uses smart contracts to make billing for freight automatic. This is done to solve these problems. Since this method makes it possible to instantly check, authenticate, and align bills, no one has to get involved, and conflicts are less likely to happen. The smart contracts on the site make sure that everyone agrees on the terms and conditions of the shipment, including the price, any extra fees, and how to pay.

By using this system based on distributed ledger technology (DLT), Walmart Canada has gained a lot of important benefits. Starting with the main benefit, putting in place automatic billing and reconciliation has greatly cut down on administrative costs and delays. Additionally, the use of smart contracts ensures accurate calculation of both set and variable fees, which lowers the likelihood of mistakes and disputes. Also, being able to track and check bills in real time makes things more clear

[6] `https://www.hyperledger.org/case-studies/dltlabs-case-study`

and builds trust between everyone involved. This led to Walmart Canada and its shipping partners saving a lot of money because there were fewer disagreements and more efficiency.

Tokenization

Tokenization in Asset Ownership

Distributed ledger technologies (DLTs) have been used by Ava Labs to tokenize asset ownership. The main goals of the company are to improve operational efficiency, make products more accessible to new customers, and increase liquidity. Wu, CEO of Ava Labs, talked about how important immediate settlement is, which is not possible with traditional methods. Because the blockchain is open and public, blockchain settlements let buyers see where their assets are stored on the blockchain. Clearing processes can also be carried out right away.

Distributed ledger technologies (DLTs) were used by Ava Labs to create a blockchain-based system that stores assets as tokens. In turn, this made it easier to create a digital ticket that can be sent, kept, and traded safely. There were three things going on at the same time during the tokenization process: technical, legal, and business. As part of the technical track, Solidity was used to build a smart contract that holds the coin. It was easier to create, manage, and trade tokens thanks to this smart deal.

As part of the court process, the token was given legal rights. This meant making a link between the object, the token, and the owner. This can be done in a number of ways, some of which require less trust than others. This part of the process made sure that the token was legal and accurately showed a real right to the underlying asset.

As part of the business track, investors were given the newly created coin in exchange for a fee. A digital platform that allows secondary trading was used, which meant that commercial efforts had to be made to sell the token.

The tokenization project by Ava Labs shows how distributed ledger technologies (DLTs) can change the way traditional financial markets work. Using blockchain technology, the group has created a better, more secure way to show who owns an object and transfer that ownership. Digital ledger technologies (DLTs) have also opened up new ways to share assets, improved liquidity, and lowered costs. Other businesses that want to tokenize assets and use the benefits of blockchain technology can look at this project as a model.

dApps

Chainlink is a decentralized oracle network that runs on the Ethereum blockchain as a dApp. It gives smart contracts a safe and reliable way to connect to external data sources, APIs, and payment systems. Chainlink's decentralized network of nodes makes sure that data is correct and can't be changed, which makes it an important part of many DeFi apps.

Another example is Brave, a web browser that gives users Basic Attention Tokens (BAT) for viewing ads. Brave is based on the Ethereum blockchain, and the token awards system is run by a decentralized application (dApp). The decentralized application (dApp) lets marketers, publishers, and users, who are all important parts of the advertising ecosystem, take part in a new way of making money that rewards people for their attention.

Distributed ledger technology (DLT) has been added to the dApp EOS Dynasty. Based on the EOS blockchain, this is a role-playing game. People who play this game can make heroes, gather materials, and fight to earn tokens. A decentralized program (dApp) is used by the game to run the token economy. This lets players trade tokens and earn rewards.

Distributed ledger technology (DLT) and a decentralized application (dApp) have been combined to make MakerDAO. The system works on the Ethereum blockchain and is a decentralized credit tool. It lets people set up collateralized debt positions (CDPs) and make Dai, a stablecoin whose value is tied to the US dollar. A decentralized lending platform is made possible by the decentralized application (dApp), which lets users get loans in the form of Dai by using their collateral as protection.

Cloud Providers Integrating DLTs

Distributed ledger technologies have the power to completely change many businesses, and cloud providers are becoming more and more aware of this. Because of this, they are using these tools in their work to provide cutting-edge solutions.

For example, TD SYNNEX Public Sector has built a group of strategic partners to provide cloud services to government departments and higher education institutions. Their cloud solutions team at TD SYNNEX Public Sector offers many services, including hosting safe apps, making and testing apps quickly, handling a lot of data, and storing it in different ways. Organizations can take advantage of a more simplified and effective approach to IT management by utilizing the cloud's capabilities.

The CODEvolved platform, a private Platform-as-a-Service (PaaS) service from the company, is a great example of how DLTs can be integrated into cloud solutions without any problems. CODEvolved gives developers the freedom to focus on writing code for new application services while also giving IT operations teams a flexible and dependable infrastructure platform. Red Hat's OpenShift Enterprise private PaaS is available on this platform. It runs on Amazon Web Services (AWS) servers. It provides a setting for developing applications that is both flexible and fully set up. Due to the use of DLTs, CODEvolved makes application creation and deployment much more collaborative and streamlined.

Cloud service companies such as AWS, Microsoft Azure, and Google Cloud Platform (GCP) have also begun to include DLTs in their offerings. AWS, for instance, offers a blockchain service that allows users to build and manage blockchain networks. This service makes sure that data storage and transaction handling are safe and clear. Azure has a blockchain development kit that lets developers use blockchain technology to make cutting-edge apps. This lets them use the full potential of distributed ledger technology. GCP offers a blockchain platform that lets users build, run, and manage blockchain networks. This makes it possible to use blockchain technology in a way that is both flexible and secure.

These cloud service providers use DLTs to provide cutting-edge solutions for many fields, including healthcare, identity verification, and supply chain management. In supply chain management, DLTs can be used to keep an eye on materials and goods all the way through the chain, making a clear and safe record of all interactions.

DLTs can help with identity verification because they make it easy to create safe digital IDs. People will be able to control their personal data, and private data will be kept safe. DLTs are a reliable way for the healthcare business to store and manage electronic health records. This technology lets healthcare workers get accurate and up-to-date information while protecting the privacy of patients.

Adding DLTs to cloud services is a dynamic and ever-changing field that always shows new use cases and uses. Because technology is always getting better, we can expect a lot of new, ground-breaking solutions that use DLTs to change many different businesses. Cloud service providers are at the forefront of this trend because they provide the technology and tools needed to make DLT-based solutions and put them into action. Businesses and groups will work very differently from now on because DLTs are becoming more popular. Digital ledger technologies will soon play a big role in making data transfers safe, clear, and quick.

Success Factors and Lessons Learned from Decentralization and Integrating DLTs into Business Operations

The recent years have seen a notable increase in the popularity of decentralization and the use of distributed ledger technologies in corporate operations. As more businesses use these technologies, it is critical to identify the critical success drivers and the insightful knowledge their implementations provide.

Success Factors

After a thorough examination of multiple sources and an analysis of real-world instances, it is apparent that a few critical characteristics are essential for the successful integration of DLTs into company operations:

Decentralized System (Protocol)

To keep the DLT network secure and intact, a decentralized system is necessary.

Transparency in Data Information

Transparency in data is essential to building trust and accountability within the DLT network.

Ensuring Data Immutability

To avoid unwanted changes and protect the integrity of the data stored on the DLT network, it is essential to maintain data immutability.

Increasing Data Security and Reliability

Protecting the integrity and confidentiality of the data that is stored on the DLT network is of the utmost significance.

Providing Full Traceability

In the DLT network, full traceability is essential to upholding transparency and accountability.

Lessons Learned

The following are some insightful discoveries made possible by the incorporation of DLTs into corporate operations:

Digital Innovation

In order to successfully deploy DLTs in company operations, it is essential to embrace digital innovation.

Information Management and Smart Contracts

These two components are essential to ensuring the safe and efficient operation of DLT networks.

Intelligent Construction

Intelligent construction is essential to ensuring DLT networks' scalability and flexibility.

Methods and Techniques in Data Analytics

The application of data analytics methodologies and strategies is critical to deriving meaningful insights from the data housed in DLT networks.

The elements of success and the important lessons learned from integrating distributed ledger technologies into company processes are demonstrated by a plethora of real-world examples. Just like we discussed, Walmart has improved the efficiency and openness of its supply chain management by implementing a DLT-based system to track food goods from farm to fork. In a similar line, Estonia's deployment of a blockchain-based digital identity management system has greatly improved the security and effectiveness of its government services.

In the end, integrating DLTs into business processes successfully requires careful consideration of the critical components for success and knowledge gathered from earlier deployments. Businesses may ensure the effective implementation of DLTs and benefit from decentralization and transparency by understanding these variables and lessons.

CHAPTER 9

Regulatory Considerations in Decentralized Cloud Solutions

When businesses decide to integrate decentralized cloud solutions into their operations, they need to think about a number of legal issues. Moving to cloud services, enterprises should think about a number of issues, such as security, data governance, outsourcing/vendor management, business continuity, and keeping records.

User-Controlled Data Sharing

User-controlled data sharing is an important part of distributed cloud platforms. It gives users fine-grained control over their data and lets them share certain data with certain people. Users can stop logging in at any time, which makes sure that no one else sees their data without their permission.

G. Deshmukh and S. M. Thameem Nizamudeen, *Decentralized Business*,
https://doi.org/10.1007/979-8-8688-0953-8_9

Controlled by the user access control is essential for data sharing in distributed clouds. It allows users to set permissions for their data, which makes sure that only authorized users can see or change it. Entry management is needed to stop unauthorized entry, data leaks, and other security risks. Users can be sure that their data is safe and that only authorized people can view it by setting up access control.

A lot of different access control methods can be used with distributed cloud systems. The person who owns the data has full control over who can access it, which is called discretionary access control (DAC). The owner can let anyone in or keep them out at any time. According to mandatory access control (MAC), the system administrator sets the rules that control who can access what. Users are given a security clearance level that tells them if they can view data or not. In role-based access control (RBAC), users' access is based on what they are supposed to do at work. User roles are assigned, and based on those roles, data access is given or denied.

Attribute-based access control (ABAC) is another paradigm that is becoming more common in distributed cloud apps. In this way of thinking, access control is built on a group of factors related to the user, the data, and the environment. Access is either given or denied based on a set of rules that evaluate those traits. ABAC is more flexible and scalable than other access control methods. In the healthcare field, for example, ABAC can be used to give healthcare professionals access to patient data based on the type of data, their position, and their jobs.

There are many other types of access control methods that can be used in distributed cloud systems besides access control models. ACLs, or Access Control Lists, are groups of rights that are linked to a property. They spell out what can be done and who can use the resource. Users are given codes, or capabilities, that tell the system what they can do with a resource. This is called capability-based access control. Public key infrastructure, or PKI, is a way to verify a user's identity using public key cryptography, which lets them access resources.

In decentralized clouds, user-controlled data sharing gives users full control; thanks to selective data sharing, users can share specific data traits, like their name, email address, or location, without sharing the entire dataset.

To share certain types of data selectively, advanced data encryption methods are used. These include attribute-based encryption (ABE) and homomorphic encryption. With the help of these techniques, only authorized parties can see certain characteristics. As an example, a user might encrypt their data so that only healthcare professionals can see their medical information.

Strong security measures should be a top priority for governments. Data encryption, which can be done with algorithms like RSA-2048 and AES-256, is a very important way to protect the private information that is saved on the ledger. This makes sure that the data can't be read even if someone gets access without permission.

Consent Management

Consent management is the process of getting and keeping track of user permission to share data. It is an important part of user-controlled data sharing because it makes sure that users know about and agree to the terms and conditions of data sharing. Consent management means telling people how their data will be used, shared, and kept safe in a clear and reliable way.

Consent forms, which detail the specifics of data sharing, are frequently used to handle consent. Users must directly agree to share their data, and they should be able to take back their agreement at any time. Consent management also involves giving users the chance to review and change their consent preferences as needed after any changes to the terms and conditions of data sharing are made.

Transparency and Auditing

Because they make users aware of how their data is being used and shared, transparency and checks are crucial to user-controlled data sharing. Transparency means giving people clear, concise information about how personal data is used, shared, and protected. Auditing means keeping track of and recording actions that access and share data to make sure they follow user permission and data protection rules.

To make things clear and easy to check, modern logging and tracking tools, like blockchain-based ones, are used. These technologies let people keep a clear, unchangeable record of how their data is being used and shared, and they also let people track and watch how data is being accessed and shared in real time.

There are laws and regulations that have been put in place to make sure that users can control how they share data on decentralized cloud platforms. Providers must follow data protection laws, such as the GDPR (General Data Protection Regulation), which is used across the whole of the European Union, and the CCPA (California Consumer Private Act), which is upheld by the Civil Code of the State of California.

Decentralized cloud storage providers must also follow security laws and standards that are specific to their business in order to keep user data secure. The Health Insurance Portability and Accountability Act (HIPAA) was a federal law that required the creation of national standards to keep private health information about patients from being shared without their knowledge or consent. These standards were followed by the Payment Card Industry (PCI) standards, which are used to handle credit cards from major card brands and other financial data.

Data Privacy

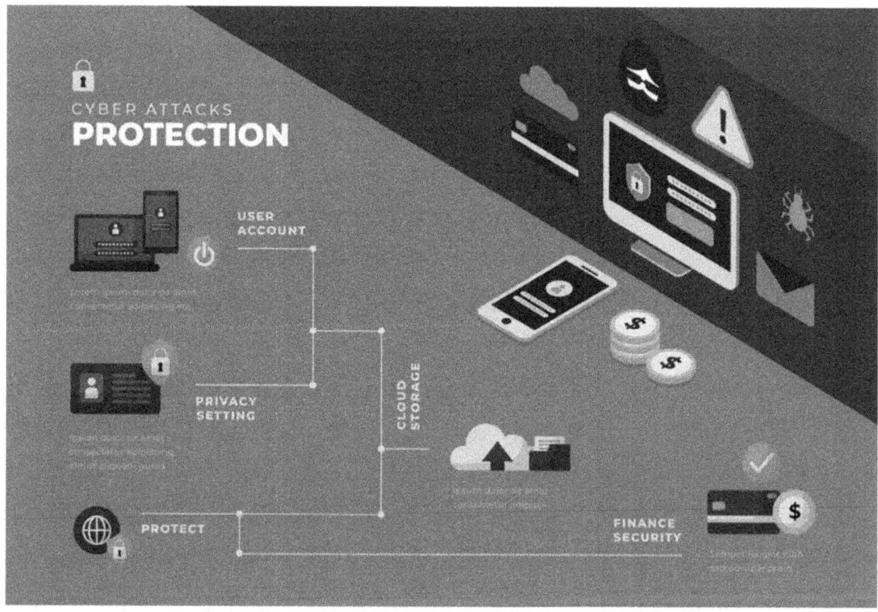

***Figure 9-1.** Different types of data that need protection*

There are a number of privacy laws that businesses need to keep in mind when they use decentralized cloud options. Complying with privacy and data protection rules like the General Data Protection Regulation (GDPR) and the California Consumer Privacy Act (CCPA) is an important thing to think about. To keep private data safe, this includes a number of steps, such as reducing the amount of data stored, encrypting it, and controlling who can see it. Businesses must also set up the right procedures to handle requests from data subjects, such as those who want to see, change, or delete their personal data.

When businesses work with decentralized cloud providers to handle personal data, they should make sure that their data processing agreements spell out exactly what each party's role and responsibility is. This includes making it clear what the goal of the data processing is, what kinds of data are being handled, and what security measures are being used to keep the data safe. By signing this agreement, everyone involved will fully understand their roles and tasks when it comes to protecting personal data.

One important thing to think about is the location needs of the data. Businesses should be aware of data localization rules, which may say that personal data needs to be stored and processed in a certain country. This is very important in decentralized cloud computer settings, where data may be stored and processed in different regulatory regions. Businesses must make sure they strictly follow these rules to avoid any legal or regulatory problems that might come up.

Businesses have to follow rules about how to notify customers of a data breach, if there is one. In the event of a security breach, this means telling the right people and government bodies. To make sure they are ready for a breach, organizations should set up incident response plans and processes for breach reporting. Ensuring this includes fully understanding the breach, successfully stopping it, and quickly telling those affected and regulatory agencies about it.

Businesses need to think about the need for data portability and connectivity, which could mean moving personal data easily between different platforms and systems. This is very important in decentralized cloud computing settings, where data can be saved and processed on many different platforms and systems. To follow these rules, businesses must make it easy for personal data to move between different systems and platforms.

Businesses should also think about the need to delete personal information and change names. To protect people's privacy, personal data may need to be de-identified or given a fake name. This is very important in decentralized cloud computing settings, where data can be sent and handled on different platforms and systems. To protect people's privacy, businesses must make sure that privacy-protecting measures are used, such as data anonymization and pseudonymization.

Standards for data openness and responsibility should be a top priority for businesses. Personal data may need to be handled in a way that is both clear and responsible. To make sure that privacy and data protection rules are followed, steps like data protection impact assessments (DPIAs) and data protection officers (DPOs) must be put in place. Businesses can make sure that their decentralized cloud solutions follow data security and privacy rules by thinking about these regulatory factors.

The FedRAMP program is a well-known example of how the government controls data that is handled and kept in the cloud in the United States. FedRAMP is a simplified version of the Federal Information Security Modernization Act (FISMA), which is a US law that controls how federal agencies and their contractors process and store data. It was made for cloud-based installations and is part of a larger set of rules meant to make sure that IT systems are safe and reliable.

Furthermore, in the UK, all organizations that are based in or process data from the UK must follow the UK GDPR and the Data Security Act 2018.

Jurisdictional Issues

Businesses that use decentralized cloud computing systems have to navigate a complex network of governmental regulations in order to stay in line and avoid legal problems. It is important for personal data to be kept and processed in a certain area because of data localization. In decentralized cloud systems, where data may be spread out across different countries, this criterion is very important. Businesses need to make sure they follow the rules for data translation to avoid legal and regulatory problems.

Limits on moving personal data across borders stop personal data from moving outside of a certain region. When businesses use decentralized cloud systems that need to send data between different countries, they must follow these rules.

Additionally, companies need to know the rules and laws that apply to their autonomous cloud solutions in every place where they do business. This means knowing how the legal and regulatory systems work and knowing how to settle disagreements when there are problems with the legal or regulatory systems. Making sure that regulations are followed is very important because companies may have to follow different laws in different places.

In decentralized cloud systems, data protection authorities are very important, and businesses need to know what their job is and what power they have in each jurisdiction. When working with decentralized cloud settings, international data transfers are very important to think about because they often involve moving data across national borders. Organizations need to fully understand the laws and rules that guide sending data between countries and take the necessary steps to make sure they are followed.

Businesses can make sure that their autonomous cloud solutions follow the rules in their area by carefully looking at these regulatory factors. This way, they can avoid any legal or regulatory problems. However, to successfully navigate this complicated terrain, you need to have specialized knowledge. Businesses should form partnerships with legal and regulatory professionals to make sure they understand the requirements and take the right steps. Businesses can get the most out of decentralized cloud computing while minimizing legal and governmental risks by carefully planning their IT needs and following the rules.

The first lessons on how to deal with problems in different jurisdictions are decentralized cloud systems, which are studied in schools. For instance, the problems with Microsoft Ireland and Google Pennsylvania show that cloud management needs to be broken down into three parts: storage location, company access, and cloud management.

Decentralized cloud storage services should try to follow these laws and let their customers know about any updates or changes. As decentralized cloud storage and Web3 technologies become more popular, regulatory systems are changing to adapt to their unique pros and cons.

Decentralized Identity Management

There are some legal problems that companies should consider when they want to use decentralized identity management in decentralized cloud systems. Decentralized identity management systems require strong safeguards against hacking and unauthorized entry because they store private information about users. This means to follow all data protection laws and put in place strong security means to protect user data. It includes things like encrypting data, setting up rules on who can access it, and regularly checking the security.

It takes a lot of people and processes to make decentralized identity management solutions work. In other words, systems must be able to communicate with each other and follow the same rules. Groups like the W3C should have businesses as members so that they can help make open standards and make sure that different systems can easily work together. Users will be able to easily move their digital identities from one identity management system to another thanks to this feature.

Companies must also follow rules like Know Your Customer (KYC) and Anti-Money Laundering (AML) rules to make sure they know who their buyers are. Decentralized identity management systems must be developed in order to satisfy these needs. There may need to be safe ways to check someone's identity for this to work. When businesses do this, they can cut down on scams and make sure they are following the law.

The ownership and control of data are important parts of independent identity management. With decentralized identity management systems, users typically have full control over their own digital IDs. Businesses need to make sure that their solutions keep users' information safe and have clear ways to handle data. It is important for customers to understand how their data is gathered, stored, and used. They should also be able to manage their own digital identity.

Businesses should also set up ways to check that decentralized identity management solutions are open and follow the rules set by lawmakers. Setting up audit records, tracking tools, and incident response systems is part of this process. These help find and fix security problems. One way for businesses to make sure that people and groups are accountable for what they do is to set clear rules for how to do so.

Businesses and the government should work together to make sure that decentralized identity management systems follow the new laws and rules. This means giving feedback on how new rules are made, taking an active role in business working groups, and talking to regulatory groups in an open way. To make sure that decentralized identity management systems are safe and legal and protect users, groups and government officials can work together.

There are not yet any specific laws that cover decentralized identity management in a broad way. Still, laws and rules in place now, like GDPR and CPRA, give DI (decentralized identity) systems a way to protect data and keep it private. As DI technology keeps getting better, new rules and laws are likely to be made to deal with the unique benefits and problems that come with decentralized identity management.

Smart Contract Regulations

When businesses deal with smart contract rules in decentralized cloud systems, they need to think about a number of legal issues. Smart contracts have been an idea for a while, but they have only recently become possible to use in real life thanks to progress in blockchain technology. Blockchain is a distributed digital ledger that keeps track of all events and shows them in order of when they happened. However, the legality of smart contracts is still not clear in some places, and companies need to stay up to date on changes in the law to make sure they follow it.

Interoperability and following standards are very important for smart contract laws. Multiple people and systems may be involved in decentralized cloud solutions, so they need to be compatible and standardized. Businesses should join industry working groups like the W3C to help shape open standards and make sure that different systems can work together easily. With this feature, users will be able to easily switch between different cloud systems, and their smart contracts will be safe and portable.

Businesses have to follow the rules when it comes to identity verification. Smart contracts need to be made in a way that follows KYC (Know Your Customer) and AML (Anti-Money Laundering) rules and protects users' privacy and safety. Businesses should also make sure that their solutions are designed to stop fraud before it happens and fully follow all the rules that apply.

Regulations for smart contracts require that there be ways to check and hold people accountable. To find and fix security problems, businesses should set up audit trails, recording tools, and incident response processes. Establishing clear accountability methods is one way for businesses to make sure that people and groups are responsible for what they do.

Legally, smart contracts are contracts, and state and federal courts enforce them the same way they enforce any other contract. Smart contracts, on the other hand, run automatically, so regulation probably won't be needed. If someone breaks a smart contract, all the solutions that work for regular contracts would apply.

Some regions have passed "smart contract laws," but that doesn't mean that blockchain smart contracts are automatically legally binding contracts. A lot of states are trying to figure out if smart contracts can be used as legally binding documents.

Estonia has been a leader in digital identity management, and its e-identity system is thought to be one of the most advanced in the world. The United States does not have a federal contract law. Instead, each state decides how to understand and enforce contracts. In this way, smart contracts have different legal standing in different places. Some US states, like Wyoming, Arizona, and Nevada, have passed laws that recognize and regulate smart contracts that are built on blockchain. Arizona, for example, wants to pass a law that would let businesses use blockchain-based smart contracts, and Wyoming has already passed a law that says smart contracts are legally binding.

Businesses should work with regulators to make sure that the limits on smart contracts are in line with new rules and laws. This includes giving feedback on how new rules are made, actively taking part in business working groups, and having open conversations with regulatory organizations. Businesses and government agencies can work together to make sure that smart contract laws are safe and followed and protect users' privacy and freedom.

Smart contract security is also very important. Governments should make sure that these contracts are safe and don't have any flaws. In order to do this, one could review and test the code, use safe coding methods, and build on safe libraries and frameworks. This promises dependability and execution, as you would expect from a smart contract, without any security concerns.

Governments should also set up security systems like GDPR, PCI-DSS, and HIPAA to make sure that the DLT system follows all relevant laws and rules. This makes sure that the system meets the requirements for protecting data and privacy, and it was made with these components in consideration.

When data leaks or security breaches happen, governments need to be ready with an incident reaction plan. This plan should include what to do after a security event, such as actions to contain the problem, get rid of it, and get back to normal. This makes sure that the government is ready to move quickly and strongly if there is a security issue. Regular security checks should also be done to find and fix holes in the DLT system.

CHAPTER 10

Future Trends

The Intersection of Cloud and Decentralized Technology

Decentralized cloud computing is more than just a buzzword; it is a genuine paradigm shift that is gaining traction in many different sectors. And with good cause: thorough research and fresh approaches like Ethernity Cloud encourage it.

What then is the significance? Improved security, scalability, and efficiency are the goals of decentralized cloud architecture. Distribution of data throughout a network of endpoints helps us to lower latency, increase performance, and cut costs. It also removes single points of failure, which makes it much harder for cybercriminals to get your data. For example, Impossible Cloud keeps your data safe and GDPR-compliant while nevertheless using distributed architecture to offer a service that is up to 80% less expensive than traditional providers.

The shift to distributed cloud computing represents a strategic path toward digital autonomy, cost savings, and enhanced data security, not only technical development. Decentered clouds offer a practical, future-proof substitute as businesses and governments seek to retake ownership of their digital assets. Leading the way in this transformation are companies like Impossible Cloud, which highlight the sensible advantages of distributed architecture via significant cost savings, improved performance, and robust data security practices. As this technology develops, it should change the scene of cloud computing and increase its accessibility, security, and efficiency for businesses all around.

G. Deshmukh and S. M. Thameem Nizamudeen, *Decentralized Business*,
https://doi.org/10.1007/979-8-8688-0953-8_10

Let's learn about several emerging innovations poised to revolutionize the way we interact with the Internet and utilize cloud computing in the realm of Web3.

Edge Computing

Edge computing is a new technology that is changing how we connect with the Internet and use cloud computing. Including IoT and AI, 5G, and smart cities, this new discovery has the potential to fundamentally affect many different sectors. The details of edge computing will be discussed in this session together with its advantages and ability to change our way of life and business.

In contrast to relying on centralized clouds or data centers, edge computing is a distributed computing paradigm that pushes computation and data storage closer to where the data is produced. By cutting the distance the data must go through, this approach reduces latency, accelerates real-time processing, and increases speed.

Traditional cloud computing sends data from sensors or devices to a centralized cloud or data center for processing and analysis. This results in increased security concerns, bandwidth congestion, and too-slow latency. Edge computing turns this around by processing data closer to the source, at the "edge" of the network. Edge devices, including routers, gateways, and even cellphones, will help in accomplishing this.

Edge computing has the potential to change how we utilize the cloud and connect to the Internet. By processing data nearer to its source, edge computing reduces latency, enhances real-time processing, and increases performance. Applications needing real-time computing—including IoT, artificial intelligence, and 5G—especially benefit from this approach.

Edge computing's main benefit is its ability to help lower the amount of data that has to be transferred to the data center or cloud. Processing data at the edge could help us lower the volume of data that has to be sent, therefore lowering the bandwidth requirements, network congestion, and costs.

It reduces the amount of data transported to the cloud or data center, therefore enhancing security. Processing data at the edge helps us to reduce the risk of data leaks while nevertheless guaranteeing that sensitive information is handled and stored safely.

Edge computing's ability to do real-time processing and decision-making adds still another benefit. Edge computing brings data closer to the source, decreases latency, and enables real-time processing and decision-making. Applications requiring real-time processing, such as smart cities, industrial automation, and self-driving cars, among others, benefit significantly from this.

Decentralized Data Network

A decentralized data network is a distributed system enabling data storage, management, and sharing free from central authority or middleman. Decentralized data networks save and handle data across an online connected network of nodes—devices, computers, or servers, among other things. Data is mirrored over several nodes in this distributed architecture, thereby guaranteeing data availability even if one node fails, thus increasing the durability and fault-tolerability of the system.

These networks have the potential to change the way we use cloud computing and interact with the Web3. These networks are meant to be distributed; hence, they run without a central authority or mediator. Rather, data is kept and controlled over a network of nodes—devices, computers, servers—linked via the Internet.

New application cases, including distributed artificial intelligence (DeFi) and distributed social networks, should surface as technology develops. The possibility of distributed data networks to provide more security and privacy is among its main benefits.

Decentralized data networks make it more difficult for hackers to access and alter data by spreading it over several nodes. Since data is encrypted and access is controlled by cryptographic keys, decentralized network systems can also offer more private and secure data exchange. For sectors like finance and healthcare that demand great degrees of confidentiality and anonymity, distributed data networks are a tempting solution.

For data administration and interchange, decentralized network architectures offer a more flexible and scalable option. Decentralized data networks can rapidly grow to satisfy the needs of growing businesses or applications since extra nodes can be added or deleted as needed. Moreover, decentralized data networks can run more independently when nodes make decisions based on their own policies and procedures. This lets data networks run more effectively and efficiently, hence removing the intermediary or central authority required.

Decentralized data networks are a fundamental element of the distributed Internet in Web3. They help to create decentralized apps (dApps) free from middlemen, therefore fostering a more democratic and inclusive Internet in which users own their data and identities.

By enabling a distributed cloud computing architecture, decentralized data networks have the ability to challenge the conventional cloud computing paradigm in terms of cloud computing. By allowing network nodes to provide computing resources, storage, and bandwidth, a distributed cloud computing paradigm produces a peer-to-peer (P2P) network that is more resilient, safe, and affordable. This approach will make cloud computing resources more available to people and companies so they may participate in the network and get incentives for their contributions.

Serverless Computing

Serverless computing is a way of using the cloud that has become more popular in the past few years. In this model, the cloud provider manages the infrastructure and gives out computing resources based on what is needed. Customers don't have to set up and run their own servers. With this approach, developers can focus on writing code and putting apps online without having to worry about the technology underneath.

One thing that makes serverless computing unique is that it is based on events. Serverless functions are set off by events like HTTP requests, changes to the database, or reports from the message queue. These functions only last a short time, usually between milliseconds and minutes, and their job is to finish a certain work. When the job is done, the function ends and the tools are made available again.

Some of the most well-known serverless computing systems are AWS Lambda, Azure Functions, Cloud Functions, OpenWhisk, and Fn. For serverless computing, these platforms come with many features and tools, like the ability to work with different computer languages, connect to other cloud services, and have security and monitoring built right in. Serverless computing can be used for many things, like processing data in real time, API gateways, background tasks, chatbots, and voice aides.

Serverless computing works great with Web3 because it lets developers make apps that are safe, scalable, and cheap and can communicate with decentralized systems.

One of the best things about serverless computing in Web3 is that it lets users and decentralized apps (dApps) connect with each other in real time and based on events. Without the need for complex infrastructure management or scaling, serverless computing allows developers to build dApps that respond to user interactions in real time. This makes the user experience smoother and easier to understand, which is very important for Web3 technologies to be widely used.

The way we use cloud computing in the setting of Web3 will also change thanks to serverless computing. In traditional cloud computing models, developers set up and handle the infrastructure, which can take a lot of time, cost a lot of money, and lead to mistakes. Developers can concentrate on making apps rather than managing infrastructure thanks to serverless computing, which eliminates these problems. This speeds up the development process, cuts costs, and improves scalability, all of which are important for making and launching Web3 apps.

One important thing about serverless computing is that it can do data processing and analytics without a central server. Without the need for centralized data warehouses or processing centers, serverless computing enables developers to build apps that can handle and analyze massive amounts of data in real time. This lets data processing and analytics work in a more free and democratic way, which is important for building trust and openness in Web3 apps.

In the framework of Web3, serverless computing is also creating new ways to make money and run businesses. Instead of using conventional subscription-based models, serverless computing allows developers to build applications that make money through token economies. This makes it possible to make money in new ways, which is very important for making Web3 apps that last and can be expanded.

Serverless computing also makes it possible for new Web3 uses and apps, like decentralized finance (DeFi) and non-fungible tokens (NFTs). DeFi applications that support real-time lending, borrowing, and trading without the use of conventional financial intermediaries can be made using serverless computing by developers. In the same way, serverless computing makes it possible to create non-fungible tokens (NFTs), which are unique digital assets that can be bought, sold, and traded on open markets.

Cloud-Native Applications

If you want to use the scalability, freedom, and reliability of cloud computing, you can now make a new kind of app called a cloud-native app. These apps were made with cloud-based tools and services in mind, and they are meant to run in the cloud infrastructure. A microservices architecture is often used to build cloud-native apps. This architecture breaks the app up into smaller, separate services that can be built, deployed, and scaled separately.

Modern computer languages and frameworks, like Java, Python, and Node.js, are often used to make cloud-native apps. These apps are meant to use cloud-based services like serverless computing, containerization, and service mesh. DevOps techniques like continuous integration and continuous deployment (CI/CD) are often used to launch these apps. These techniques make it possible to add new features and updates quickly and often.

Developers can make cloud-native apps that are built from the ground up to work with the cloud infrastructure. This lets them give users faster, safer, and more flexible experiences.

When more people use decentralized applications (dApps), they can grow to meet their needs. This is one of the main ways that cloud-native apps are changing how we use Web3. The scalability of traditional apps is often limited by the infrastructure that supports them. This can lead to poor performance, downtime, and unhappy customers. Cloud-native apps, on the other hand, are made to expand horizontally, adding or removing resources as needed to meet shifting demand. This means that dApps can handle a lot of traffic and user activity while still running quickly.

Web3 experiences are also becoming more interactive and immersive thanks to cloud-native apps. Utilizing cloud-based services like augmented reality (AR) and virtual reality (VR), developers can make cloud-native apps that merge the real and digital worlds into engaging, interactive experiences.

For example, cloud-native apps are being used to create virtual events and experiences where users can interact with digital items and each other in real time. This gives people new ways to socialize, have fun, and learn.

Cloud-native apps can support machine learning and real-time data processing. Using cloud-based services like data lakes and machine learning platforms, cloud-native apps can look at huge amounts of data in real time. This lets developers learn more about user behavior, tastes, and needs. This lets developers make experiences that are personalized and flexible so they can meet the needs of each user. This makes the experience more interesting and successful for all users.

The way we use cloud computing will also change because cloud-native apps will make it easier to automate, organize, and control cloud resources. Cloud-native tools and platforms let developers automate the deployment, scaling, and control of cloud resources. This lets them focus on writing code instead of managing infrastructure. This helps developers get their work done faster, save money, and make their apps more reliable and safe.

Lastly, cloud-native apps make it easier for people to work together and come up with new ideas when making Web3 apps. By using cloud-based services like open-source platforms and developer groups, cloud-native apps let developers from all over the world share knowledge, resources, and code to make new and interesting apps. This lets developers use the knowledge of people all over the world, which cuts down on development time and costs and speeds up growth in the Web3 ecosystem.

Hybrid Cloud Strategies

Hybrid cloud strategies combine infrastructure or apps that are on-premises with services that are in the cloud to make a single, unified environment. In this way, businesses can get the best of both worlds: they can use the cloud's scalability and flexibility while keeping the resources they already have on-premises. Hybrid cloud solutions can be put into practice in a number of different ways, such as using cloud-based services for some workloads or apps and keeping others on-premises or using cloud-based infrastructure to help with on-premises capacity during times of high demand.

Multi-cloud plans, on the other hand, use more than one cloud provider to meet the needs of different businesses or to avoid being locked into one seller. Employing this method lets companies use the best features and strengths of different cloud service providers, like Amazon Web Services (AWS) for AI and machine learning, Microsoft Azure for business software and apps, and Google Cloud Platform (GCP) for data analysis and machine learning. There are different ways to use multiple clouds. For example, you can use different cloud providers for different workloads or applications, or you can use a single cloud provider for a certain market or area.

One of the best things about hybrid cloud methods is that they can make experiences consistent and unified across many settings. By combining on-premises infrastructure or apps with cloud-based services, businesses can create a single platform. Workloads, data, and applications can be easily moved between locations because of this. That way, businesses can use the cloud's scalability, freedom, and low cost while still keeping control and safety over private data and programs.

Another big benefit of hybrid cloud methods is that they can help you get the most out of your resources while also cutting costs. When companies use cloud-based services for non-core jobs or changing workloads, they can free up on-premises resources for important applications and save money at the same time. Also, mixed clouds let businesses use cloud-native services like AI, machine learning, and the Internet of Things (IoT), which can help them be more innovative and competitive. Hybrid clouds are also the basis for edge computing, which processes and analyzes data in real time at the edge of the network, reducing latency and improving performance.

Multi-cloud strategies are structured on the hybrid cloud approach by letting businesses use more than one cloud provider to meet their unique needs. Companies can avoid being locked into one provider, save money, and become more flexible and scalable by using this method. Businesses can pick the best cloud provider for each application or workload based on cost, speed, and security with a multi-cloud approach. Businesses can also use cloud-native services and new ideas from different sources with this method, which makes them more flexible and competitive. Multi-cloud solutions also make it possible for apps and services that don't depend on a specific cloud to be used and controlled across multiple clouds.

More hybrid and multi-cloud methods are being used, which is also leading to new ideas in cloud management and automation. Businesses will need better tools and platforms to handle and coordinate their cloud systems as they put these plans into action. Because of this, cloud management platforms (CMPs) and cloud orchestration tools have been made to help businesses control and handle cloud resources, apps, and services in a variety of settings. These technologies give businesses a way to handle all of their cloud resources from one place. This lets them make the best use of their resources, save money, and boost security and compliance.

The Future

Projected trends show a big shift toward hybrid and multi-cloud settings as cloud and decentralized technologies get better. It is expected that by 2025, more than 90% of businesses will use a hybrid cloud approach that combines public, private, and edge clouds to meet their unique business needs. They will make this change because they want more freedom, scalability, and cost-effectiveness, and they also don't want to be locked into one vendor.

The future of cloud computing will also be significantly influenced by decentralized technologies such as Bitcoin and distributed ledger technology. More than half of cloud-based apps will likely use autonomous technology by 2027. This will give users more security, freedom, and openness. This will be clearest in fields like banking, healthcare, and supply chain management, where honesty, trustworthiness, and openness are very important.

In the future, edge computing and 5G networks will make it possible for a new wave of decentralized, self-driving, and AI-powered cloud-based services and apps. Edge computing will handle more than 75% of all cloud-based workloads by 2030. This will allow processing, research, and decision-making to happen in real time at the network edges. This will have a big effect on fields that need fast and low-latency transmission, like the Internet of Things, self-driving cars, and smart cities.

CHAPTER 11

Conclusion

Navigating the Web3 Landscape

The Dawn of a Decentralized Future

Throughout this book, we have looked at the transformational potential of Web3 and decentralized technologies, from grasping the core principles of DLT to examining its implementations in the real world and future trends, keeping in view the radical impact these technologies are about to unleash upon industries and features that characterize our digital lives.

As we conclude, let us briefly summarize some of the critical concepts and insights that have shaped our understanding.

Web3 is a paradigm shift in the way we use the Internet from a centralized platform dominated by technology giants to one that is more decentralized and user-centric. This allows users to take better control of their data, identity, and digital assets.

DLT, and more so blockchain, forms the bedrock on which Web3 is built.

Because DLT allows secure, transparent, and tamper-proof recording of data, a digital environment can be created where a trustless, verifiable system can be established.

G. Deshmukh and S. M. Thameem Nizamudeen, *Decentralized Business*,
https://doi.org/10.1007/979-8-8688-0953-8_11

Smart contracts are agreements that execute automatically once predefined rules encoded on a blockchain have been met, potentially automating business processes in many sectors and reducing intermediaries in a manner that could drive a system with increased efficiency, cost-effectiveness, and security.

Charting a Course Through Decentralized Cloud Solutions

The meld of Web3 and cloud computing opens vistas of innovation never explored before. The decentralized cloud solutions based on DLT overcome the shortcomings of traditional models of centralization by disseminating data and computational resources across a network of nodes.

Decentralized storage alternatives like IPFS and Filecoin are increasingly being adopted, as they offer significantly enhanced security, affordability, and resistance to single-point failures. These offer dispersed networks of suppliers of storage in order to eliminate dependency on centralized data centers and all risks of data breaches, censorship, and vendor lock-in.

Not only that, but DLT is also transforming cloud computing in many aspects, from secure data storage and supply chain management to identity verification and dApps. It is the creation of tamper-proof records, automation of agreements through smart contracts, and establishing mechanisms for decentralized trust that will transform how businesses will interact and function online.

Embracing the Future: Trends Shaping Web3 and Cloud

A trend of Web3 and further down to the road of decentralized technologies could be obtained, which indicates that a future is at hand where such innovations will be integrated into the very fabric of cloud computing.

With the increasing proliferation of IoT devices and the rollout of 5G networks, edge computing will play the most pivotal role in enabling real-time processing at the network edge. This distributed computing paradigm enhances efficiency, reduces latency, and unlocks new possibilities for applications requiring instantaneous data analysis, such as autonomous vehicles, smart cities, and industrial automation.

Decentralized data networks have become an integral part of the applications in Web3. In general, they introduce users to the concept of direct ownership of their data and give way to security and transparency in data. These networks, therefore, can build a more balanced and democratic Internet where data is owned by the people.

Serverless computing, owing to its event-driven nature and abstraction in managing infrastructure, will revolutionize cloud computing in the perspective of Web3. It empowers not only developers to be more agile to focus on application logics without caring about infrastructures but also enables scalability and cost efficiency that will speed up the development and deployment of innovative applications over Web3.

Cloud-native applications are fit for the cloud and will help drive the ecosystem of Web3 forward. Specifically, building applications on top of microservices architectures and applying DevOps principles will provide the much-needed scaling, resiliency, and agility required for dApps to grow their user bases and adapt to evolving demands.

Hybrid cloud strategies will balance on-premises infrastructure with cloud-based services and provide the organizations with a balanced approach toward leveraging the strengths of both worlds. Such flexibility within this model empowers them to save costs, enhance security, and tap into a wider range of cloud-native services with their critical data and applications in their full control.

Sailing Through the Web3 Frontier

Standing at the threshold of a decentralized future, it should be decisively stated that Web3 and decentralized technologies are in a state of evolution and continue to evolve. Of course, this path ahead will no doubt be with challenges and opportunities, all of which require adaptation, innovation, and responsible development.

Embracing the values of decentralization, transparency, and user empowerment will enable us to unlock the full transformational power of Web3 in building a fairer, safer, more innovative digital future. The adventures into this decentralized future have just begun, and the potential will be endless.

Index

A

ABAC, *see* Attribute-based access control (ABAC)
ABE, *see* Attribute-based encryption (ABE)
Access Control Lists (ACLs), 120
ACLs, *see* Access Control Lists (ACLs)
AI2, *see* Artificial intelligence (AI)
Alphabet Inc. (Google), 14
Amazon Web Services (AWS), 35, 60, 113, 135, 139
APIs, *see* Application Programming Interfaces (APIs)
Application Programming Interfaces (APIs), 55, 61, 65, 112
Ark project, 25
Artificial intelligence (AI), 2, 15, 132
Attackers, 76, 77
Attribute-based access control (ABAC), 120
Attribute-based encryption (ABE), 121
Auditing, 122
AWS, *see* Amazon Web Services (AWS)

B

Basic Attention Tokens (BAT), 112
BAT, *see* Basic Attention Tokens (BAT)
BFT, *see* Byzantine fault tolerance (BFT)
Binance Smart Chain (BSC), 61
Bitcoin, 25
Bittensor, 41
Blockchain, 4, 6, 72, 73, 100, 143
  built-in system, 17
  challenges, 22–25
  cryptocurrencies, 17
  definition, 17
  vs. DLT, 20–22
  information tracking, 17
  "state of disorder", 25
Blockchain applications
  identifying information, 19
  patient data maintenance, 20
  PII, 19
  tracking public ledger, 19
  tracking real estate deals, 19
Blockchain-based digital identity management system, 117
Blockchain-based energy, 99
Blockchain-based IoT solutions, 13

G. Deshmukh and S. M. Thameem Nizamudeen, *Decentralized Business*,
https://doi.org/10.1007/979-8-8688-0953-8

Blockchain-based LC solutions, 106, 107
Blockchain-based transactions, 18
Blockchain-based voting system, 108
Blocks, 3
BSC, *see* Binance Smart Chain (BSC)
Byzantine fault tolerance (BFT), 73

C

California Consumer Privacy Act (CCPA), 79, 123
California Consumer Private Act (CCPA), 122
Capability-based access control, 120
CCPA, *see* California Consumer Privacy Act (CCPA); California Consumer Private Act (CCPA)
CDPs, *see* Collateralized debt positions (CDPs)
Centralized cloud architecture, 34
Centralized cloud computing, 35
Centralized platform, 4
Centralized *vs.* decentralized consensus, 72
Chainlink, 112
Cloud-based monitoring services, 62
Cloud computing, 33, 136, 138
  DLT applications
    data management and storage, 38
    electronic data storage with features, 38
    financial transactions and payment processing, 39
    managing user IDs and permissions, 38
    supply chain management, 38
  DLT use case
    dApps, 45, 46
    financial services, 47, 48
    healthcare, 47
    identity verification, 45
    IoT, 48
    secure data storage, 44
    smart contracts, 44
    supply chain management, 44, 45
    tokenization, 46
    voting systems, 47
  future, 141
  traditional, 132
Cloud management platforms (CMPs), 140
Cloud-native apps, 137, 138, 145
Cloud orchestration tools, 140
Cloud service providers, 114
Cloud services, 34, 60
Cloud storage providers, 35
CMPs, *see* Cloud management platforms (CMPs)
CODEvolved platform, 113

Collateralized debt
positions (CDPs), 112
Companies, 33
using DLT
Alphabet Inc., 14
Amazon, 14
IBM, 13
Toyota, 14
Walmart, 14
Comprehensive testing, 66
Computer languages, 137
Computer network rules, 21
Consensus algorithms, 22
Consensus mechanism, 72
Consent forms, 121
Consent management, 121
Controlled blockchain
network, 21
Corda, 58
Cortex, 40
Create, Read, Update, and
Delete (CRUD), 4
Cross-DLT communication, 71
CRUD, *see* Create, Read, Update,
and Delete (CRUD)
Cryptocurrency blockchain, 76
Cutting-edge solutions, 114

D

DAC, *see* Discretionary access
control (DAC)
DAG, *see* Directed acyclic
graph (DAG)
DAOs, *see* Decentralized
Autonomous
Organizations (DAOs)
dApps, *see* Decentralized
applications (dApps)
Data analytics, 35, 116–117
Data block, 17
Data tampering, 82–84
dBFT, *see* Delegated Byzantine fault
tolerance (dBFT)
DBFT, *see* Democratic Byzantine
fault tolerance (DBFT)
DDoS, *see* Distributed Denial-
of-service (DDoS)
Decentralization, 2, 5
Decentralized applications
(dApps), 5, 45, 46, 85,
112, 137
Decentralized Autonomous
Organizations
(DAOs), 95, 97
Decentralized Bitcoin
exchanges, 19
Decentralized blockchains, 21
Decentralized cloud computing,
34, 35, 131
advantages
cost effectiveness, 39
data ownership and
control, 39
enhanced scalability, 39
enhanced security, 39
DLT, 34
objectives

Decentralized cloud computing (*cont.*)
  affordability, 36
  enhanced competition, 36
  enhanced security, 37
  no monopolized control, 35
  quality services, 36
  reliability, 36
  storage and power-sharing, 37
  user's privacy protection, 36
 peer-to-peer cloud marketplaces, 34
Decentralized computing, 93
Decentralized data networks, 133, 134, 145
Decentralized finance (DeFi) systems, 6, 90, 93
Decentralized future, 146
Decentralized governance, 93
Decentralized identity management, 93
Decentralized infrastructure, 34
Decentralized storage, 144
 cloud professionals
  DLT cloud architect, 96
  DLT cloud engineers, 96
  DLT consultants, 97
  DLT security specialists, 97
  smart contract developers, 96
 content changes, 91
 decentralization/redundancy, 91
 deduplication, 91
 P2P network, 91
 privacy/security, 92
 use cases, 92
 versioning/mutability, 92
Decentralized storage solutions
 advantages, 50
 competitive environment, 50
 cryptographic proofs and smart contracts, 49
 dispersed network, individual contributors, 48
 dynamics, 50
 economic benefit, 48
 individual storage nodes, 48
 inherent robustness, 50
 peer-to-peer strategy, 48
 replication, 49
 risk reduction, 50
 safeguarding and securing data, 49
 traditional cloud storage providers, 51
Decentralized systems, 94, 95
 consensus, 72
 interoperability, 70
 privacy, 74, 75
 scalability, 69
Decision-making, 133
Delegated Byzantine fault tolerance (dBFT), 74
Delegated proof-of-stake (DPoS), 74

Democratic Byzantine fault tolerance (DBFT), 74
Denial-of-service (DoS), 78, 80
Digital cryptography, 18
Digital database, 3
Digital innovation, 116
Digital ledger technologies (DLTs), 112, 114
Directed acyclic graph (DAG), 20, 71
Discretionary access control (DAC), 120
Distributed artificial intelligence, 133
Distributed Denial-of-service (DDoS), 64
Distributed ledger technologies (DLTs), 29, 67, 69–71, 73, 110–113
  applications, 8
  blockchain, 4, 12
  business value, 6, 7
  CRUD execution, 4
  cutting-edge technologies, 15
  decentralized nature, 4
  financial industry, 7
  records and property maintenance, 4
Distributed networks, 3
DLT-based smart contracts, 30
DLT for entrepreneurs
  finance, 9
  government and public sector, 11
  healthcare, 10, 11
  internal process organization, 8
  logistics, 9, 10
  registering partnership business transactions, 8
  supply chain management, 10
DLT implementations, 20
DLT integration, cloud-based infrastructure
  considerations
    cloud provider and infrastructure, 64
    monitoring and maintenance, 65
    security, 64
    smart contracts, 65
    testing and validation, 65
    uninterrupted connection, 65
  delpoyment and monitoring, 62–64
  designing DLT network, 59, 60
  developing smart contracts, 60, 61
  platform selection (*see* DLT platform selection)
  testing and validation, 61, 62
  use case identification, 54
DLT platform selection
  Corda, 58
  ETH, 55, 56
  factors consideration, 55
  Hyperledger Fabric, 57
  Quorum, 59
  requirements-based, 55

DLTs, *see* Digital ledger technologies (DLTs); Distributed ledger technologies (DLTs)
DoS, *see* Denial-of-service (DoS)
DPoS, *see* Delegated proof-of-stake (DPoS)

E, F

Edge computing, 132
  ability, 133
  benefit, 132
  and 5G networks, 141
eID card, 101
eID system, 101, 102
ELCP, *see* Ethereum Light Client Protocol (ELCP)
Erasure coding, 49
Ethereum (ETH), 37, 55, 56, 77, 88
Ethereum Light Client Protocol (ELCP), 56
Etherscan, 63
Etherscan API workflow, 63
EU Blockchain Forum, 30
Everledger's blockchain, 10

G

GCP, *see* Google Cloud Platform (GCP)
GDPR, *see* General Data Protection Regulation (GDPR)
General Data Protection Regulation (GDPR), 75, 79, 122
General Licensing and Business Practices Act (GLBA), 74
Gensyn, 42
GLBA, *see* General Licensing and Business Practices Act (GLBA)
Google Cloud Platform (GCP), 113, 139

H

Healthcare, 47
Health Insurance Portability and Accountability Act (HIPAA), 74, 122
HIPAA, *see* Health Insurance Portability and Accountability Act (HIPAA)
Hybrid cloud methods, 139
Hybrid cloud strategies, 138, 145
Hyperledger Fabric, 57, 110

I, J, K

IAM, *see* Identity and Access Management (IAM)
IBM, 13
Identity and Access Management (IAM), 79
IDS, *see* Intrusion detection systems (IDS)

Individual shocks, 24
Information technology (IT), 15
Intelligent construction, 116
Inter Blockchain Communication (IBC) protocol, 25
International cooperation, 30
Internet of Things (IoT), 48, 104
Interoperability, 70
Intrusion detection systems (IDS), 63
IoT, *see* Internet of Things (IoT)
IOTA Tangle, 71
IT, *see* Information technology (IT)

L

LCs, *see* Letters of Credit (LCs)
Leased proof-of-stake (LPoS), 74
Legacy transaction networks, 24
Letters of Credit (LCs), 106
LogCortex Labs, 40
LPoS, *see* Leased proof-of-stake (LPoS)

M

MAC, *see* Mandatory access control (MAC)
Machine learning (ML), 2
Mandatory access control (MAC), 120
Medchain, 109
Metaverse, 40
ML, *see* Machine learning (ML)
Modex Blockchain Database, 25
Multi-cloud methods, 140
Multi-cloud strategies, 140
Mutable links, 92

N

Network latency, 69
NFTs, *see* Non-fungible tokens (NFTs)
Non-fungible tokens (NFTs), 90, 97
Normal contract, 27
Normally, non-fungible tokens (NFTs), 92

O

Open Web Application Security Project (OWASP), 78
Orchards, 24
Ornua ran, 106
OWASP, *see* Open Web Application Security Project (OWASP)

P

Payment Card Industry (PCI), 122
Payment Card Industry Data Security Standard (PCI DSS), 74
PBFT, *see* Practical Byzantine fault tolerance (PBFT)
PCI, *see* Payment Card Industry (PCI)

PCI DSS, *see* Payment Card Industry Data Security Standard (PCI DSS)
Peer-to-peer network, 80
Peer-to-peer transactions, 6
Permission/private blockchain, 21
Personally identifiable information (PII), 19
PII, *see* Personally identifiable information (PII)
Platform-as-a-Service (PaaS) service, 113
PoET, *see* Proof-of-elapsed time (PoET)
PoS, *see* Proof-of-stake (PoS)
PoW, *see* Proof-of-work (PoW)
PoWeight, *see* Proof-of-weight (PoWeight)
Practical Byzantine fault tolerance (PBFT), 74
Private blockchain networks, 24
Proof-of-elapsed time (PoET), 74
Proof-of-stake (PoS), 73, 74
Proof-of-weight (PoWeight), 74
Proof-of-work (PoW), 73, 74
Public blockchain networks, 21
Public-key cryptography, 6
Public land record system, 102, 103

Q

Quorum, 55, 59

R

Randomized proof-of-stake (RPoS), 74
RBAC, *see* Role-based access control (RBAC)
RBFT, *see* Redundant Byzantine fault tolerance (RBFT)
Redundant Byzantine fault tolerance (RBFT), 74
Regulatory challenges, 29–32
Replication, 49
Resilience, 50, 62, 86
Richline Group Inc., 15
Role-based access control (RBAC), 120
RPoS, *see* Randomized proof-of-stake (RPoS)

S

Satoshi Nakamoto, 18
SDKs, *see* Software Development Kits (SDKs)
Secure Software Development Framework (SSDF), 78
Security information and event management (SIEM), 63
Security monitoring tools, 63
Security risk
- 51% attack, 77
- data tampering, 82–83
- smart contracts, 78, 79
- Sybil attack, 80–81

Semantic web, 2
Serverless computing, 135, 136, 145
Sharding, 69
Sidechains, 69
SIEM, *see* Security information and event management (SIEM)
Smart contracts, 19, 44, 75, 78, 88, 110
  deal terms, 27
  description, 27
  DLT, 28
  independent, 28
  public blockchains, 30
  regulatory issues, 29
  security and openness, 28
  simple transactions, 29
  transaction records, 28
Software Development Kits (SDKs), 57
SSDF, *see* Secure Software Development Framework (SSDF)
State channels, 69
Storj and Siacoin, 37
Success drivers
  data immutability, 115
  DLT network, 115
  full traceability, 116
  integrity and confidentiality, 116
  transparency, 115
Sybil attack, 80–81

T

TD SYNNEX Public Sector, 113
Tokenization, 46, 111
Toyota Motor Corporation, 14
TradeLens blockchain, 23
Traditional contracts, 26
  vs. smart contract, 28
Traditional *vs.* decentralized computing, 34
Transparency, 122
Trust Anchors, 23

U

Ubrich, 9
US-based Amazon.com, 14
User-controlled data sharing, 119

V

VE, *see* Virtual Enterprises (VE); Virtual Environments (VE)
Vending machines, 26
Virtual Enterprises (VE), 70
Virtual Environments (VE), 71
Voatz, 107, 108
Voting nodes, 73
Voting systems, 47

W, X, Y, Z

Walmart, 14
Walmart's Food Tracking System, 104

Web 1.0, 1
Web 2.0, 1
Web3, 85, 137, 145, 146
  and cloud computing, 144
  dApps creation, 86, 87
  and decentralized technologies, 143, 146
  digital assets, 90
  new ownership, 90
  smart contracts, 88
  transactional models, 90
Web 3.0
  aim, 1
  AI/ML, 2
  integrated communication framework, 1
  vs. Web3, 2

www.ingramcontent.com/pod-product-compliance
Lightning Source LLC
LaVergne TN
LVHW051640050326
832903LV00022B/827
* 9 7 9 8 8 6 8 8 0 9 5 2 1 *